Current Issues in the Law of Evidence

Editor: A. Keith Thompson

SHEPHERD
STREET PRESS

Published in 2021 by Connor Court Publishing Pty Ltd under the imprint Shepherd Street Press.

Shepherd Street Press is an imprint of Connor Court Publishing and The School of Law, The University of Notre Dame Australia, Broadway.

Shepherd Street Press Editorial Executive:

Michael Quinlan
A. Keith Thompson
Iain T. Benson

Connor Court Publishing Pty Ltd
PO Box 7257
Redland Bay QLD 4165
sales@connorcourt.com
www.connorcourtpublishing.com.au
Phone 0497-900-685

Printed in Australia

ISBN: 9781922449702

Front Cover Image: Themis. Wikipedia Commons: pixabay free images.

Peer Review Policy
This book has been prepared in compliance with the Peer Review Policy of the Shepherd Street Press which provides for double blind peer review by at least two expert reviewers.

The editors also wishes to acknowledge the assistance they have received from Jesse Gibson, a final year Honours student. Among other tasks, Jesse has assisted in ensuring compliance with the fourth edition of the Australian Guide to Legal Citation.

Table of Contents

Introduction

James B. Thayer and John H. Langbein have both observed that the law of evidence is the law of jury control.[1] And yet in the lay mind, the jury is closely aligned with the delivery of civil rights because it has so often been called 'the bulwark of liberty'. The law of evidence itself has connections with civil rights because the presumption of innocence, the privilege against self-incrimination and the right to competent legal representation in a criminal trial have been picked up in many national constitutions and international human rights instruments and have arguably become a part of customary international law. But in a Westminster democracy that does not have a constitutionally entrenched Bill of Rights like Australia, the creation of a statutory law of evidence does not provide any long-term protection for such human rights. Indeed, as ordinary legislation, the law of evidence can be amended or repealed by a simple majority vote in parliament even when dictated by a moral panic, and the consolidation of evidence laws in one place arguably makes it more likely that these rights will be taken away because they are thus identified as part of the legislative domain.

The vulnerability of common law and human rights protections which were developed in English custom to protect persons accused of crime, may be demonstrated in a variety of ways, including the following three. First, absent the protection of human rights in the *Australian Constitution*, the principle of legality expresses the well settled principle that the legislature can take away any common law or human right Australians have

---

1   James B. Thayer, "The Jury and Its Development III", *Harvard Law Review*, Vol. 5, No. 8, 357, 387-388 and John H. Langbein, "The Origins of Public Prosecution at Common Law", *The American Journal of Legal History*, Vol. 17, No. 4, 313, 317.

previously enjoyed, provided it does so with clear and unambiguous words.[2] Examples where such rights have been removed by Australian legislatures include the right to cross-examine those who accuse someone of sexual assault,[3] the right not to incriminate oneself,[4] the right to confidentially confess sins against children to a religious practitioner[5] and the right to a legal representative of one's choice.[6]

---

2   See for example French CJ in *Momcilovic v The Queen* (2011) 245 CLR 1 [46]-[47] where he said:

> The principle of legality has been applied on many occasions by this Court. It is expressed as a presumption that Parliament does not intend to interfere with common law rights and freedoms except by clear and unequivocal language for which Parliament may be accountable to the electorate. It requires that statutes be construed, where constructional choices are open, to avoid or minimise their encroachment upon rights and freedoms at common law…It protects, within constitutional limits, commonly accepted ''rights' and 'freedoms'…The common law 'presumption of innocence' in criminal proceedings is an important incident of the liberty of the subject. The principle of legality will afford it such protection…as the language of the statute will allow…Nevertheless, statutory language may leave open only an interpretation…which infringe one or more rights of freedoms. The principle of legality…is of no avail against such language.

3   So-called rape shield laws vary from state to state in Australia. In New South Wales, s 293 of the *Criminal Procedure Act 1986* provides that evidence relating to the sexual reputation of the complainant is generally inadmissible, though that may be overcome if the probative value of such evidence would outweigh 'any distress, humiliation or embarrassment that the complainant might suffer as a result of its admission.'

4   For example, though the self-incrimination privilege was not completely abrogated by s 155(7) of the *Trade Practices Act 1974* (Cth) in *Pyneboard Pty Ltd v Trade Practices Commission* (1983) 152 CLR 328, s 6A of the *Royal Commissions Act 1902* (Cth) was sufficiently explicit to abrogate the whole of the privilege in *Sorby v Commonwealth* (1983) 152 CLR 281.

5   See for example, s 127(2) of the *Evidence Act 2011* (ACT), s 127 (2) of the *Evidence Act 2008* (Vic) and s 14(7) of their *Children, Young Persons and Their Families Act 1997* (Tas).

6   For example, ss 29, 39 and 46 of the *National Security Information (Criminal and Civil Proceedings) Act 2004* (Cth) 'provide that parts of a proceeding may not be heard by, and certain information may not be given to, a lawyer for the defendant who does not have the appropriate level of security clearance' ("Right to a lawyer", *Australian Law Reform Commission*, July 31, 2015 < https://www.alrc.gov.au/publication/traditional-rights-and-freedoms-encroachments-by-commonwealth-laws-alrc-interim-report-127/10-fair-trial/right-to-a-lawyer/>, [10.119]. See also the decision in *K-Generation Pty Ltd v Liquor Licensing Court* (2009) 237 CLR 501 where the High Court of Australia upheld provisions of s 28A of the *Liquor Licensing Act 1997* (SA) which prevented the applicant knowing the case against him to the extent it required disclosure of 'criminal intelligence' and his lawyers could not know the

Second, despite the double jeopardy principle which was a principal element in Catholic Archbishop Thomas Becket's dispute with King Henry II, there is no current limit on how many times the state may bring a criminal case before a jury, provided no previous jury could agree whether to convict or acquit the accused. The only practical impediment to retrial in the case of a hung jury, is the state's assessment of the likelihood of securing a conviction in any retrial. The consequence in the *Murphy*, *Pell* and *Hayne* cases, is that the prosecution may learn what works and what does not in argument and take a different approach on second and subsequent occasions. The accused never has that option, and seldom has the resources to manage a criminal trial as in American television trials like those portrayed in the series named *Bull*.[7] Though there has been no significant research into the nature and practice of jury vetting in Australia and though it is said to be prohibited in Victoria by the de-

---

case either unless the court approved that the information be shared on the provision of suitably undertakings on pain of contempt. Similar conclusions followed the consideration of West Australian legislation in *Gypsy Jokers Motorcycle Club Inc v Commissioner of Police* (2008) 234 CLR 532.

7   In *Dietrich v R* (1992) 177 CLR 292 (Brennan and Dawson JJ dissenting), the High Court found that to ensure a fair trial, the trial judge should have adjourned the case against Dietrich until counsel had been found to act for him. Though there was no common law right for him to have counsel paid for from the public purse, since there was a chance of complete acquittal in his case (the jury had already acquitted him of one charge when the trial proceeded without defence counsel (ibid 39 per Mason CJ and McHugh J)), it was essential that Dietrich be represented. Some of the majority judges went further and generalised fair trial principle. Mason CJ and McHugh J said:

[I]t should be accepted that Australian law does not recognize that an indigent accused on trial for a serious criminal offence has a right to the provision of counsel at public expense…[but] lack of representation may mean that an accused is unable to receive, or did not receive a fair trial (ibid 311).

Deane J said:

[T]he prosecution has available all the resources of government…If an ordinary accused lacks the means to secure legal representation…he will, almost inevitably, be brought to face a trial process for which he will be insufficiently prepared and with which he will be unable effectively to cope. In such a case, the adversarial process is unbalanced and inappropriate (ibid 335).

Gaudron J added:

[T]he requirement of fairness…has been recognized as independent from and additional to the requirement that a trial be conducted in accordance with law…every judge in every criminal trial has all powers necessary or expedient to prevent unfairness in the trial (ibid 363-364].

cision in the *Katsuno* case, all that decision prohibits in practice is the Chief Commissioner of Police from sharing conviction information from Police records about potential jurors until the day of the trial.[8] It does not prevent many other kinds of prosecution jury vetting in Australia and expressly does not apply to the jury vetting practices in Western Australia, the Northern Territory and Tasmania which were disclosed to the Court by intervenors representing those governments.[9] Given the poor track record of the Victorian Police in obedience to the spirit of the law when their profound illegality cannot be seen,[10] it is unlikely that the *Katsuno* decision has stopped all jury vetting practices in that state.

Third, the idea that the establishment of a *Uniform Evidence Law* in Australia would standardise the law of evidence through the continent, and perhaps protect the rights and privileges of those accused of crime, has not been realised. For not only have Western Australia, South Australia and Queensland declined to join the scheme, but the scattergun state and territory legislative responses to recommendations of the Royal

---

8   *Katsuno v The Queen* (1999) 199 CLR 40 [25] per Gaudron, Gummow and Callinan JJ. McHugh and Kirby JJ dissented and considered the prohibition should have been expressed more broadly and should have invalided Katsuno's conviction. Gleeson CJ said that 'the unlawfulness' in this case was the provision of 'the names of those on the jury panel in advance of the trial…The practical effect of what was done was to give the prosecution advance knowledge of information that could lawfully have been communicated later, and in sufficient time to enable it to be used in making a decision as to a peremptory challenge' (ibid [6]).

9   Ibid [73] per Kirby J.

10   See for example *DPP v Marijancevic; DPP v Preece; DPP v Preece* (2011) 33 VR 440 where the DPP appealed a ruling by the trial judge that 'affidavits relied on to obtain warrants had not been sworn in breach of s 81 of the Act, and accordingly found the search warrants were invalid and that the entries, purportedly pursuant to the warrants, were unlawful and constituted a trespass.' The Victorian Court of Appeal upheld the trial judge's finding that 'the gravity of th[is] impropriety was of the highest order' and 'reflected the general behaviour of members of the crime squads of the Victoria Police at the relevant time' (ibid [2], [63] and [69]. The Court of Appeal also deplored what they called 'the endemic practice employed within certain sections of Victoria Police of not requiring the accuracy and truthfulness of the contents of affidavits in support of warrants to be sworn on oath or by affirmation' (ibid [53]). Recent revelations about Victoria Police engagement of criminal barrister Nicola Gobbo as a police informant, suggest that endemic impropriety in Victoria Police practice is not a thing of the past and that the culture which concerned the Victorian Court of Appeal has not been resolved.

Commission into Institutional Responses to Child Sexual Abuse that religious confession privilege should be abrogated in child sexual abuse cases,[11] have fractured the uniformity that had been achieved.

There are also questions whether the Australian Royal Commission's recommendation that religious confession be abrogated was necessary at all since the earlier Ryan Commission in Ireland had not recommended mandatory reporting of child abuse out of respect to victims,[12] and because no cases of institutional child abuse in churches after the year 2000 had been reported to the Australian Royal Commission.[13] Given that context, it is doubtful that Article 18(3) of the *International Covenant on Civil and Political Rights* required the abrogation of religious confession

---

11   The ACT has amended its version of the *Uniform Evidence Act* and subsection 2
      now reads:
      Subsection (1) does not apply if
         (a) the communication involved in the religious confession was made for
              a criminal purpose: or
         (b) the religious confession includes information relating to –
              (i)   a child or young person that is experiencing, or has experi-
                     enced, sexual abuse or non-accidental physical injury: or
              (ii)   a substantial risk that a child or young person may experience
                     sexual abuse or non-accidental physical injury.
      This amendment avoids inconsistency with the mandatory reporting now re-
      quired of heads of religious bodies now required under the *Ombudsman Act 1989*
      (ACT). Section 127 (2) of the *Evidence Act 2008* (Vic) has been similarly amended
      and s 184 of the *Children, Youth and Families Act 2005* (Vic) also makes persons
      in religious ministry mandatory reporters. New South Wales, Tasmania and the
      Northern Territory have not made similar amendments to s 127 of their versions
      of the *Uniform Evidence Act* though they have passed mandatory reporting laws
      for religious ministers in other legislation.
12   Parents, guardians, doctors, nurses and many other people working with children
      are exempt from the Irish reporting requirements if, for bona fide reasons, they
      do not believe it would be in the best interests of the child to report the matter
      (*Criminal Justice (Withholding of Information on Offences against Children and Vulnerable
      Persons) Act 2012* (Ireland), <http://www.irishstatutebook.ie/eli/2012/act/24/
      enacted/en/html>.
13   Though the Australian Royal Commission did not discuss why very few cases of
      child sexual abuse in churches after 1990 were reported, the reasons appear to be
      a combination of internal efforts made by churches to solve the problem and the
      success of a state scheme begun in Queensland and operative from 2000 which
      prohibited anyone engaging an employee or a volunteer to work with children be-
      fore they had been cleared by an extensive police background check.

privilege as the Australian Royal Commission said it did. Rather, that recommendation presents as an orchestrated effort to set the minds of non-believing Australians public against religious freedom and belief generally, and against the religious practices of Roman Catholics in particular.

Despite the gradual implementation of the *Uniform Evidence Law* through the Commonwealth[14] after commitments made at Council of Australian Government (COAG) meetings in the early 1990s, and despite many COAG meetings after the Royal Commission released its recommendations, the states have all responded to that Commission's recommendations in different ways. The result has been that the uniformity which had been achieved in evidence law through much of the country in response to those 1990s aspirations[15] is unlikely to be restored. New South Wales' record of amendments since it signed onto the uniform scheme in 1995 illustrates the trend. For while rape shield laws were introduced by amendments to the *Criminal Procedure Act 1986* (NSW) and preserved the overall integrity of the uniform evidence regime, New South Wales Attorney-General Greg Smith subsequently introduced a new s 89A into the *Evidence Act 1995* (NSW) designed to abrogate the common law right to silence of those accused of crime, and one of his successors Mark Speakman has completely reconstructed the tendency and coincidence provisions of the New South Wales legislation to make it easier to convict those accused of sexual offences against children.[16]

---

14   The Commonwealth and New South Wales passed their versions of the *Uniform Act* in 1995. Tasmania passed its version in 2001, Victoria in 2008, and the Australian Capital and Northern Territories in 2011.

15   The Australian Law Reform Commission summarised the efforts to harmonise evidence law throughout Australia in its 102nd report in 2010 ("The movement towards a uniform evidence law", 16 August 2010 <https://www.alrc.gov.au/publication/uniform-evidence-law-alrc-report-102/2-the-uniform-evidence-acts/the-movement-towards-a-uniform-evidence-law/<).

16   The *Evidence Amendment (Tendency and Coincidence) Act 2020* came into effect on 1 July 2020 and is to be reviewed by 30 September 2022. Given that the purpose of the legislation was to lower the bar and make it easier for prosecutors to introduce 'evidence of other allegations—or convictions—of child sexual abuse perpetrated by the accused' despite the rationale for the existing provision in

While the attempt to abrogate the right to silence has been unsuccessful for practical reasons,[17] the New South Wales amendments to the uniform tendency and coincidence regime ignore the prejudice that flows from revealing past crime during a later trial even though it is a well-accepted jurisprudential principle that previously proven crime does not prove later offences. That is, the New South Wales amendments to the previous tendency and coincidence rules present as unwise amendments that pander to vindictive elements in our society and seem to accept that permanent incarceration is the only solution to criminal behaviour despite empirical proof that even child sexual abusers can be rehabilitated if they receive the right treatment.[18]

The levers of evidence law operate like the arc of a pendulum. When the mechanisms are too loose, an unacceptable number of the guilty avoid detection and punishment and the opportunity to be redeemed by sound rehabilitation programs. When we wind the mechanisms so tightly that we convict every person guilty of crime, we convict many innocents along with them. And when the mechanisms of evidence law are wound so tight that they punish and incarcerate the innocent, there is no way to count the cost of those injustices though Ros Burnet and others have attempted to draw societal attention to some of that human damage.[19]

---

the uniform law, it is doubtful that any review will improve the rights of those accused of such crimes (The Hon. Mark Speakman, Second Reading Speech, 25 February 2020 < https://www.parliament.nsw.gov.au/Hansard/Pages/Hansard-Result.aspx#/docid/'HANSARD-1323879322-109639'>).

17   The utility of the special caution required in the presence of an Australian legal practitioner has meant that experienced criminal lawyers no longer attend their clients when in custody but reiterate their right to silence when they attend them on the phone or in private (*Evidence Amendment (Evidence of Silence) Act 2013* (NSW)).

18   Keith Thompson, "Should Religious Confession Privilege be Abolished in Child Abuse Cases? Do Child Abusers Confess their Sins?" 8 *Western Australian Jurist* (2017) 95, 110-116 where I discuss research that confirms the rehabilitation prospects for child sexual abusers are good if that rehabilitation is tailored to the individual offender.

19   Ros Burnet ed., *Wrongful Allegations of Sexual and Child Abuse* (Oxford University Press, 2016).

The solution is to educate a compassionate society that knows rehabilitation is possible if it rechannels its resources from maintaining pris-
ons into programs that redeem offenders as well as their victims. Pris-
ons in the United States hold nearly 400% more prisoners per capita
than those in Australia,[20] but as our compassion gradually dissolves in
the face of political law and order rhetoric, our results track theirs more
closely. Education about the redemption of prisoners and victims takes
commitment and time and is more difficult when the anger of victims
seeking vengeance is highlighted by the media, as if human justice required spectators at a Tudor gibbet where the prisoners are taken down
live from the noose before having their organs removed before their eyes
and the quartering process begun on a butcher's block. Though our legal
forbears began the process of outlawing cruel and unusual punishment
in 1688, we still seem to crave show trials and the public shaming and
endless punishment of all offenders afterwards, especially if they are tall
poppies.

This small collection of four articles about the law of evidence from a
small law school cannot resolve any of these current issues in the law of
evidence. But it does shed light on some and raise others readers may not
have considered.

In the first, Anthony Westenberg suggests that we should not take client
legal privilege for granted. Though it has been recognised as a fundamental right in international human rights instruments since the middle of
the twentieth century, Australian legislatures have shown an appetite to
reduce and perhaps even remove it when reformers suggest that public
health and safety would benefit. He argues that a failure to understand
the privilege's purpose has led to its decline before Australian parliaments. As part of his warning, Anthony observes the demise or dilution

---

20   "International Imprisonment Rates", *Sentencing Advisory Council, Research, statistics
      and education about sentencing in Victoria* < https://www.sentencingcouncil.vic.gov.
      au/statistics/sentencing-trends/international-imprisonment-rates>   (accessed
      March 25, 2021).

of self-incrimination, spousal and religious confession privileges as the harbingers of such change.

The other three chapters respond to increased public interest in criminal procedure and jury function as a result of Cardinal George Pell's two trials in the County Court in Melbourne and his subsequent appeals in the Victorian Court of Appeal and then in the High Court of Australia. The first of those is the reprint of an article by then Oxford Professor John Finnis in *Quadrant* magazine online. We have republished the article both because it deserves a wider audience, and because the good professor does not mince his words. Though he did not know the outcome of the High Court appeal when he wrote, readers would be justified in considering there is more than a little of the seer in his analysis. He asks quite bluntly what Chief Justice Ferguson and Justice Maxwell were thinking when they wrote their majority judgment which kept the Cardinal in gaol when it was hard for objective lawyers to believe that he had been proven guilty beyond reasonable doubt as required by Victorian criminal law.

Because many lay observers of the law have queried whether Australia should stick with the jury after a second jury got it so wrong in the *Pell* case in the Melbourne County Court, I explain how the modern Australian jury came to be. I trace it from the Norman adaptation of old Anglo-Saxon, Frankish and maybe even Swedish practices into the compilation of the Domesday book, a new and uniquely English tax register put together after the Norman conquest of England in the eleventh century. I then note how it was adapted by Henry II in the twelfth century and how imaginative Norman judges further adapted it to decision making in criminal trials 50 years later when Pope Innocent III directed that the clergy could no longer be involved in non-church trials. But I observe that the greatest innovation in forming the modern English jury may have been the result of Queen Mary's appointment of Justices of the Peace to search out and prosecute those who were killing her unpopular officials. For when the largely Protestant juries in her kingdom would not cooperate in identifying the persons they thought had committed those crimes, she required her Justices of the Peace to become prosecutors. That innovation meant that juries no longer had secret knowledge of the facts and they could no longer manipulate those facts behind closed doors. Though the *Pell* trials of 2019 and 2020 have raised questions whether juries are passed their 'use-by' date, this essay explains that the Australian jury is the product of continuous evolution and suggests that our legislators should not be afraid to reform it again to ensure it continues to deliver recognisable criminal justice in the 21st century.

There is a sense in which Mark Bonanno's further chapter about the *Pell* case builds upon that historical foundation. For Mark defends the jury even though many have questioned whether we need it in the wake of both the High Court decision in the final *Pell* appeal, and the temporary expedient of judge alone trials in response to the social distancing requirements imposed by state law in 2020 because of the Covid pandemic.

In many ways this short book is just a taster. I hope our law school will be able to collect more evidence law research in the future and publish them as a greater contribution to the public understanding of criminal justice in Australia. That is an ambitious task.

Dr A. Keith Thompson
Professor of Law
School of Law and Business
The University of Notre Dame Australia
March 26, 2021

About our contributors

Mark Bonnano is the Senior Planning and Environmental Lawyer for Canterbury Bankstown Council. He conducts the Council's Land & Environment Court development hearings and its Local Court and Land & Environment Court prosecutions. He is an Accredited Specialist in Property Law and a member for the past four years of the NSW Law Society Environment and Planning Law Committee.

John Finnis AC QC is professor emeritus at Oxford University, having been Professor of Law and Legal Philosophy from 1989 to 2010. He is a Fellow of the British Academy (Law and Philosophy sections). A barrister of Gray's Inn, he practised from 1979 to 1995 and was appointed Queen's Counsel [QC] (honoris causa) in 2017. Originally from South Australia, he was created a Companion in the Order of Australia in 2019 'for eminent service to the law, and to education, to legal theory and philosophical enquiry, and as a leading jurist, academic and author'.

Keith Thompson is a Professor at the Sydney School of Law of The University of Notre Dame Australia. He previously worked as International Legal Counsel for The Church of Jesus Christ of Latter-day Saints through the Pacific and African continent and as a partner in a commercial law firm in Auckland, New Zealand.

Anthony Westenberg is a legal officer in the Australian Public Service working in administrative law litigation. Prior to this, Anthony worked as an associate in the Migration and Refugee Division of the Administrative Appeals Tribunal and volunteered at the Aboriginal Legal Service.

1

Client Legal Privilege and the Need for a Rationale

Anthony Westenberg

I   Introduction

Client legal privilege (CLP) is a fundamental privilege in evidence law. Broadly speaking, CLP maintains the confidentiality of communication between a lawyer and client, preventing this communication from being admitted as evidence.[1] The main justification for CLP today is the 'instrumental' justification; that CLP aids the administration of justice by encouraging full and frank disclosure to a client's lawyers. Other justifications include that CLP is essential for human rights in society since a person cannot effectively protect her rights without a lawyer.

Nevertheless, CLP within Australia faces abrogation by state and federal parliaments, and wary judicial thinking regarding the privilege. The reason for CLP's abrogation is that there is a lack of understanding regarding CLP's purpose, and questions as to whether CLP assists in the administration of justice.

However, the justifications that CLP aids the efficiency of courts and

---

1   The privilege has also been expanded to cover other circumstances, for example certain situations in which a lawyer speaks to third parties. However, this paper focusses on the central tenet of CLP, that communication between a lawyer and client is confidential.

that human rights are effectively meaningless without it, do not fully answer Jeremy Bentham's 19th century critique of CLP, that it only helps 'guilty people'. Bentham argued that CLP only helps a 'guilty' person, and that someone who has not committed a legal wrong is not hurt by their lawyer giving evidence, but actually may be helped. Only someone who has committed a wrong is helped by their lawyer being unable to give evidence. The modern justifications do not clearly answer Bentham's critique. These justifications do not provide a clear purpose for the privilege which could prevent CLP being abrogated by Parliament.

Bentham's critique summarises the main points of contention against the privilege. CLP must be understood by Parliament in order to be protected, and there must be a strong basis on which to answer Bentham's critique, beyond a claim that CLP merely works. Otherwise, Parliament may well read CLP in light of Bentham's criticism and move to further limit or otherwise abrogate the privilege.

The privilege has been subject to examination by the High Court over the last century. Various High Court judges hint at reasons why CLP remains important despite Bentham's arguments and modern expressions of his criticism. They imply that CLP exists as a fundamental privilege to enforce a person's rights, and they suggest that this reason alone is an adequate answer to Jeremy Bentham.

This paper first examines the current arguments for CLP, and the need for a strong response to Bentham's criticisms of CLP and modern developments of his arguments. The paper then examines Bentham's critique, to show that the standard modern justifications do not answer it. Finally, the paper answers Bentham's critique drawing from the High Court's jurisprudence, and demonstrates that this understanding does invalidate Bentham's critique.

II   Origins of Client Legal Privilege

CLP, broadly, prevents evidence of legal advice being adduced as evidence in court.[2] CLP has two limbs, the 'litigation' limb and the 'advice' limb. Under the litigation limb, CLP prevents the admission of evidence relating to advice given by a lawyer in the course of a litigated matter. Under the advice limb, CLP prevents admission of advice given by a lawyer in regards to a non-litigated matter, such as a contract negotiation. Under ss 118 and 119 of the *Evidence Act 1995* (NSW) both limbs may also apply in regards to confidential communication to third parties in relation to the litigation or general advice.[3] The privilege is held by the lawyer's client, and the client can waive their rights under the privilege and disclose their legal advice if the client wishes.[4] The privilege is not absolute, and a court may find that a person has waived their CLP rights. For example, waiver can occur when a person seeks to disclose part of the legal advice they have received to obtain an advantage in a litigated matter while withholding disadvantageous parts of the advice. In such circumstances, a court can find that the person is acting unfairly and unreasonably and require disclosure of the whole of the advice.

While CLP is a very old privilege, its origins are unclear. A similar principle existed in Roman law.[5] In English common law the privilege was first reported in two 16th century cases.[6] In these two cases, it was accepted as already settled that a person's lawyer could not be compelled to give

---

2   J D Heydon, *Cross on Evidence*, (LexisNexis Butterworths, 9th ed, 2013) 820 [25210].

3   See also similar sections in the other Uniform Evidence Act jurisdictions.

4   Heydon, (n 2), 820 [25210].

5   The privilege first appeared in the *Lex Acilia De Repetundaris* (the 'Acilian Law Concerning Extortion') around 122/123 BC. For a translation, see Allan Johnson, Paul Coleman-Norton, and Frank Bourne, *Ancient Roman Statutes* (Lawbook Exchange, 2003); see also Justinian, *Institutes of Justinian* (J T Abdy trans, Cambridge University Press, 1876) [trans of: *Institutiones*], and see also Max Radin, 'The Privilege of Confidential Communication Between Lawyer and Client' (1928) 16(6) *California Law Review* 487.

6   *Lee v Markham* (1569) Monro 275; *Berd v Lovelace* (1576) 21 ER 33; see J Auburn, *Legal Professional Privilege: Law & Theory* (Hart Publishing 2003), 3 – 7.

evidence in relation to matters in which they had acted. The reasons for those decisions is not stated in the reports that remain, so that CLP's original purpose is unclear. At first, CLP only applied in matters where litigation was anticipated.[7] This was expanded in the 19th and 20th centuries so that all general legal advice was protected, giving rise to CLP's advice limb. The 'general advice' limb of the privilege originally protected only information or documents that were prepared or given solely in relation to legal advice, but this was later changed by statute and then in the common law so that information or documents prepared for the dominant purpose of legal advice were protected.[8]

The basis for CLP has changed through its history. One of the original bases for CLP was the lawyer's honour, meaning that a court would not force a lawyer to breach his own honour by breaking his client's confidence.[9] From the 18th and 19th centuries, judges preferred to explain that the privilege assisted in the administration of justice. This justification for CLP is called the 'instrumental justification' by many commentators. CLP is said to help the administration of justice because, when lawyers are aware of all relevant facts, they can represent their clients better and ensure that the courts are not 'clogged' with weak cases that should not have been litigated. The Australian Law Reform Commission (ALRC), following the instrumental justification, argued that the privilege served the administration of justice in four areas (in its own words):

- encouraging full and frank disclosure;

- encouraging compliance with the law – because a lawyer in possession of all the facts can more effectively provide appropriate

---

7   Ronald J Desiatnik, *Legal Professional Privilege in Australia* (LexisNexis Butterworths, 3rd ed, 2017), 14.

8   Cf. *Evidence Act 1995* (NSW) Part 3.10, Div 1; *Evidence Act 1995* (Cth) Part 3.10, Div 1; *Evidence Act 2008* (Vic) Part 3.10; *Evidence Act 2001* (Tas) ss 118 – 119, as well as *Esso Australia Resources Ltd v Commissioner of Taxation (Cth)* (1999) 201 CLR 49, which brought the Australian common law in line with the Uniform Evidence Law jurisdictions.

9   J H Wigmore, *Evidence in Trials at Common Law* (Little, Brown, & Co., McNaughton ed, 1961) vol 8, 543 – 545 [2290].

advice;

- discouraging litigation and encouraging settlement – because a fully briefed lawyer can better advise the client about their prospects in court; and

- promoting the efficient operation of the adversarial system – because a party should gather their own evidence, not merely subpoena the work done by another.[10]

In summary, the modern justification focusses on the efficiency of the courts. A person consults a lawyer, and receives prompt advice that sometimes discourages litigation. The courts are therefore not 'clogged' with weak or ineffectual cases, and clients do not fear empowering their lawyers with all the facts. If lawyers do not have to disclose what clients tell them, untrained litigants are also encouraged to consult lawyers and if cases do proceed, they are presented more quickly and competently.

Several other justifications for CLP are occasionally referenced. These include that CLP enables the efficient working of the common law's adversarial system by encouraging lawyer diligence, by encouraging selected disclosures against interest,[11] and that CLP also protects an individual's privacy.[12] These justifications reinforce the modern instrumental justification. McNicol says that the modern instrumental argument works alongside these uncommon justifications to provide

> a broad rationale which furthers and promotes both the administration of justice and an effective adversary system of litigation. Legal professional privilege is said to achieve both these objectives by, first, fostering candour and trust in the lawyer-client relationship, and secondly, protecting the information of each party from disclosure to the other side.[13]

---

10   Australian Law Reform Commission, *Traditional Rights and Freedoms – Encroachments by Commonwealth Laws*, Report No 129 (2016), 340 [12.16].

11   Australian Law Reform Commission, *Privilege in Perspective: Client Legal Privilege in Federal Investigations*, Report No 107 (2007), 51 – 52 [2.18] – [2.20].

12   Ibid, 55 – 56 [2.36] – [2.39].

13   Suzanne B McNicol, *The Law of Privilege* (LawBook Co, 1992) 48 – 49.

III   Criticisms of Client Legal Privilege

A   *Bentham*

In the late 18th century, Jeremy Bentham analysed the common law and its rules according to his utilitarian philosophy. Bentham argued that the primary purpose of law and the courts was to give justice. Bentham criticised many rules of evidence law, arguing that many of the privileges should be abolished.

Bentham criticised CLP on the basis that it only protects guilty persons from punishment. Bentham's argument was that only someone who has something to hide would not want their lawyer to give evidence. If a person was truly innocent, then that person would not worry about their lawyer giving evidence.

Bentham's argument was that, because the purpose of law is to give justice, the purpose of the courts, as the administrators of law, was also to give justice.[14] In order to reach a just outcome, courts need to examine the full circumstances of each case. To achieve this a court should have access to all relevant evidence. If a court needs all relevant evidence to achieve its purpose, evidence should only be excluded for the most serious reasons.[15] Bentham then argued that a lawyer is a trusted advisor whom a client informs regarding their matters. Lawyers are therefore key witnesses because they understand the case in full. Bentham argued that the lawyers of innocent clients should then be able to give evidence of their clients' innocence. Innocent clients would therefore not be worried about their lawyer giving evidence. According to Bentham, the only reason that a person would not want a trusted advisor to give evidence is if the client believed it would harm their case and that would only occur when the client is guilty.[16] Bentham therefore argued that the only person benefits from

---

14   Jeremy Bentham, *Rationale of Judicial Evidence* (Hunt and Clarke, first published 1823, 1995 ed) vol 5, 303.
15   Ibid.
16   Ibid, 303 – 310.

lawyers being prevented from giving evidence is a client who is guilty. CLP thus does not provide a sound reason to exclude evidence in a courtroom.

Beyond this argument, Bentham provided two further bases for his criticisms. Firstly, he argued that the only reason CLP exists is because only lawyers are appointed to become judges. As judges are former lawyers, they respect other lawyers and give them special privileges in court which they do not give to other professions. Bentham therefore argued that CLP maintained elitism in the legal profession. Though some might consider this view offensive, it is easier to understand when it is recognised that the main arguments for CLP in Bentham's time were the instrumental argument for the administration of justice, and the argument for protecting a lawyer's honour. Bentham's second argument was that a court should not permit rules and tricks to be used to conceal evidence and enable a guilty person to secure an acquittal. Bentham argued that this would defeat the court's purpose to give justice. Recognising CLP made the courts parties to a game, like fox-hunting. He suggested CLP amounted to setting a guilty person free to use their wiles and legal knowledge, and then to catch them if the court could.[17] If the guilty get away, that was alright because it was part of the game. To the contrary he argued that legal rules must have a clear justification, and should not be based on assisting guilty people and giving them a chance to get away. Bentham therefore argued that legal rules must be based around effecting the court's purpose, and should not undermine the court's purpose. According to this criticism, CLP does not facilitate the administration of justice and in fact operates to undermine the court's purpose of giving justice.

B   *Modern Critics*

In recent years, Adrian Zuckerman argued that extending CLP to protect all communications between lawyer and client was unjustified. Zuckerman argued that CLP unfairly privileged lawyers' work over the equally-important, and even similar, work of other professions. Zuck-

---

17   Ibid, 316.

erman's prime example was the similar work of tax accountants. Zuckerman argued that there was no logical reason for this distinction, and that CLP should therefore be abolished in these cases or expanded to protect other advisors doing the same work.[18] Essentially, Zuckerman's argument is an expansion of Bentham's criticism that CLP exists to give lawyers special privileges over other professions, without a logical reason for limiting the privilege only to lawyers.

Bentham's argument was also examined by Max Radin in the 1920s.[19] Radin discussed the possible sources of CLP, and its history and potential origin in Roman law. Radin focussed on Bentham's criticism, and argued that the main justifications for CLP did not answer Bentham. Radin argued that privilege does not decrease litigation as some argue, but may actually increase it. A guilty person can find 'less scrupulous' lawyers, and still engage in litigation, but runs the risk of being found out – which leads to more litigation in order to correct the wrong, give justice, and punish any unscrupulous solicitors.[20] Radin also commented that, when Bentham's argument was first released, CLP was defended on the grounds that 'the rights of all persons should be submitted with equal force to our courts of justice.' The arguments justifying CLP centred on the inability of people without legal education to present their case adequately in court. That deficit in legal knowledge could be resolved by providing access to lawyers, whose training would ensure that each case '[was] brought with nearly equal ability and chance of success under the consideration of the judge.'[21] Radin argued that this argument presupposed that each lawyer was of equal ability so that each case could be presented with equal force.[22] Radin concluded that CLP was unlikely to be abolished and should be maintained, but that there was no logical

---

18   A A S Zuckerman, 'Legal Professional Privilege – The Cost of Absolutism' (1996) 112 *Law Quarterly Review* 535, 539, as quoted and summarised by H L Ho, 'Legal Professional Privilege and the Integrity of Legal Representation' (2015) 9(2) *Legal Ethics* 163,186.

19   Radin, (n 5).

20   Ibid, 491 – 492.

21   An anonymous argument in 17 *Law Magazine* 68 (1837), as quoted in Radin, (n 5), 492

22   Radin, (n 5), 492.

answer to Bentham's criticisms.[23]

Justice Mason (as his Honour then was) also doubted the privilege's value when weighed against a court having full access to all relevant information.[24] Echoing Bentham, he opined that the exclusion of evidence did little to aid a court or a client, and suggested that the public interest in a court having all the relevant evidence might well outweigh the privilege.

C   The Modern Rationale's Failure to Answer

Bentham's criticisms must be examined in light of modern justifications for CLP. If CLP is to avoid parliamentary abrogation, CLP's modern defenders must be able to answer Bentham's critique. In the paragraphs that follow I consider whether the modern justifications do provide a solid answer to Bentham.

The first point is that Bentham's criticism rests on the belief that a lawyer's evidence will be some of the most helpful, as a lawyer is a trusted confidante. However, Bentham's criticism assumes that a lawyer's evidence would bear more weight than the evidence of another witness, and that a client would still entrust her lawyer with all the relevant facts if CLP were removed. Because it is doubtful that a lawyer's evidence would assist the court, it is also doubtful that excluding such evidence would hinder a court. However, from Bentham's point of view, this is true of all human witness evidence – the value of all evidence is unknown until it has been adduced, tested, and weighed against other evidence. It is therefore illogical to exclude lawyer evidence before it is tested in court to determine its utility.

The second point is that evidence law recognises that there are some categories of evidence which are inherently unreliable or untrustworthy,

---

23   Ibid.
24   *O'Reilly v State Bank of Victoria Commissioners* (1983) 153 CLR 1, 26 [44] – [45] (Mason J).

and these should be excluded to avoid possible injustice. When review-ing the Evidence Act 1995 (Cth), the ALRC noted that hearsay evidence was barred by policy, since it is generally unreliable and of little value.[25] If CLP were abolished and evidence of communication between lawyer and client admitted, the resulting evidence would be hearsay unless the client was also required to testify despite the right to silence. Thus be-fore evidence of communication between lawyers and their clients could be generally admitted in court, parliament would have to decide wheth-er it also wished to abrogate the right to silence for persons accused of crime and make an exception to the rule that prohibits the admission of second-hand evidence on hearsay grounds.

Despite his antipathy towards CLP, Bentham surprisingly argued that religious confession privilege was justified. He reasoned that because confession was an inherent part of Catholicism, coercing the disclosure of confessional information in court was an unjust interference with the free exercise of that religion. Bentham also argued that compelling the disclosure of confessional information would remove the salutary effects of confession, since confessions would cease to occur as soon as such a law was passed and thereafter priests would not be able to exhort or otherwise encourage penitents to repent and making reparation for their crimes.[26] Although discussing religious confessional privilege's merits or lack thereof is beyond the scope of this paper,[27] a legitimate question arises as to why Bentham did not apply the same logic to CLP? For if CLP were abolished, those accused of crime would no longer seek legal ad-

---

25 Australian Law Reform Commission, *Uniform Evidence Law*, Report No 102 (2006), 190 [7.12] – [7.13]

26 Jeremy Bentham, *Rationale of Judicial Evidence* (Hunt and Clarke, first published 1823, 1995 ed), vol 4, 586 – 592.

27 The area of religious confessional privilege is one of current debate, with differ-ent Australian jurisdictions taking their own steps in relation to this. The ALRC has argued that the privilege should be subsumed under a general confidential communications privilege (see Australian Law Reform Commission, *Uniform Ev-idence Law*, Report No 102 (2010), 524 – 525 [15.85] – [15.88]; Queensland has abolished the privilege in relation to child sexual abuse, see *Criminal Code (Child Sexual Offences Reform and Other Legislation Amendment Act 2020* (QLD) s 25, and there is further debate in this regard in other jurisdictions.

vice. Removing CLP could therefore remove any salutary benefits of legal advice, despite Bentham's argument that CLP only aids guilty people to escape justice. Removing CLP would likely also discourage law-abiding people from seeking legal advice to ensure that their business or other affairs were conducted according to the law. Applying Bentham's own logic for religious confessional privilege to CLP, it would appear reasonable to argue that the salutary benefits of legal advice outweigh its negatives. Although one could argue that these are small benefits, Bentham argued that advantage of permitting evidence of religious confession would 'be casual and even rare: the mischief produced by it, constant and all-extensive.'[28] If one accepts that a lawyer's evidence would always be second-hand and of limited value without confirmation by a silent client, then the benefit of permitting a lawyer's evidence would be small but the mischief perhaps 'all-extensive.'

It is also valid to question whether Bentham was right to conclude that a court will come to the right verdict if it receives all of the evidence. That conclusion assumes unrealistically that a court would receive all the evidence it needs to give a just verdict if CLP were abolished, but this argument is an unfair criticism of Bentham since we cannot be sure a court will give a just verdict even if it has all of the available evidence since there are other rules that will still deprive the court of evidence if CLP were abolished. Nor would the abolition of the whole law of evidence ensure just verdicts since the law of evidence is not the only impediment to the gathering of relevant evidence.

Despite these criticisms of Bentham's argument, the modern idea that CLP is justified because it aids the administration of justice by weeding out weak cases is not a complete response to Bentham's criticism. That is because weeding out weak cases is an unconvincing reason to frustrate a court's attempts to give justice in the light of all available evidence.

---

28   Bentham, (n 26), 589.

Although the ALRC and Wigmore argued that CLP reduces litigation,[29] Radin argued that it would increase litigation, as noted above. In more recent times, Desiatnik has noted that some cases before modern courts, are complicated by questions of CLP including whether the privilege has been impliedly waived.[30] Thus although one can argue that CLP has reduced litigation because it enables lawyers to encourage clients not to litigate, clients retain the option for litigation and CLP complicates that litigation in some cases when it is taken. There is also the argument that a lawyer could still advise a client not to litigate even if there was no CLP.

Finally, one can argue that CLP is important because it fosters trust between lawyer and client. While trust certainly enhances the lawyer-client relationship, that enhanced trust alone does not present as a good reason why a court should forego relevant and probative evidence as it strives to provide justice in society. That trust alone is not a sufficient reason to justify CLP is affirmed by the fact that courts in the eighteenth and early nineteenth centuries did not accept that protecting a lawyer's sense of honour was a reasonable basis for allowing CLP. It has also been observed that trust is as necessary in an accountant-client relationship as in a lawyer-client relationship and does not justify CLP if other advice obtained in trust in equivalent relationships is not similarly protected.[31]

---

29   Wigmore, (n 9), 552 [2291]; ALRC, (n 8), 340 [12.16].
30   Desiatnik, (n 5), 303.
31   This is not to say that other professions do not engage in important work; only that justifying CLP on the basis of trust does not give a clear reason as to why the lawyer-client relationship is privileged but other professional-client relationships may not be. That is also not to say that other professional relationships may never be subject to a privilege, as the law of evidence continues to develop, and there have been some attempts to provide the bases on which a new privilege may arise (see, e.g., *D v NSPCC* [1978] AC 171).

IV   Client Legal Privilege and the Administration of Justice

In light of this analysis of common rationales for CLP, one must ask whether CLP really does help the administration of justice. Some High Court judgments have addressed this question and asserted that CLP is also a fundamental privilege founded in non-derogable human rights and operates as a 'bulwark against tyranny.'

In *Baker v Campbell*,[32] Deane J stated that CLP enables persons accused of civil and criminal wrong to obtain independent legal advice, and thus protects them 'against the leviathan of the modern state.'[33] His Honour stated that the availability of independent legal advice is of particular importance to the 'weak, the unintelligent, and the ill-informed,'[34] and is necessary to enable everyone to 'cope with the demands and intricacies of modern law.'[35] In *Attorney General (NT) v Maurice*,[36] Deane J developed this argument about the need for independent legal advice and added that CLP is essential to its meaningful existence. He said:

> That general principle [of CLP] is of great importance to the protection and preservation of the rights, dignity and freedom of the ordinary citizen under the law and to the administration of justice and law in that it advances and safeguards the availability of full and unreserved communication between the citizen and his or her lawyer and in that it is a precondition of the informed and competent representation of the interests of the ordinary person before the courts and tribunals of the land. Its efficacy as a bulwark against tyranny and oppression depends upon the confidence of the community that it will in fact be enforced. That being so, it is not to be sacrificed even to promote the search for justice or truth in the individual case or matter and extends to protect the citizen

---

32   (1983) 153 CLR 52
33   *Baker v Campbell* (1983) 153 CLR 52, 120 (Deane J).
34   Ibid.
35   Ibid.
36   (1986) 161 CLR 475.

from compulsory disclosure.[37]

His Honour reiterated his support for CLP in *Waterford v The Common-wealth*.[38] Referring to the quote above,[39] he observed that CLP is founded on easing judicial administration through the independent advice of skilled lawyers, and the 'protection and preservation of the rights, dignity and freedom of the ordinary citizen under the law.'[40] In his final year on the Bench, he noted that CLP's purpose was that it played

> an essential role in protecting and preserving the rights, dignity and freedom of the ordinary citizen – particularly the weak, the unintelligent, and the ill-informed citizen – under the law.[41]

In the same case, McHugh J argued that CLP serves to enable a lawyer to

> advise [clients] of their rights under the law and, where necessary, take action on their behalf to defend or enforce those rights. The doctrine is a natural, if not necessary, corollary of the rule of law and a potent force for ensuring that the equal protection of the law is a reality.[42]

Stephen J, with Mason and Murphy JJ, noted that CLP enhanced the administration of justice by 'facilitating the representation of clients by legal advisers, the law being a complex and complicated discipline.'[43] A few years later, Justice Stephen again stated that CLP is founded upon 'the need of laymen for professional assistance in the protection, enforcement or creation of their legal rights.'[44]

---

37   Ibid, 490 (Deane J).
38   (1987) 163 CLR 54.
39   *Attorney General (NT) v Maurice* (1986) 161 CLR 475, 490 (Deane J).
40   *Waterford v The Commonwealth* (1987) 163 CLR 54, 82 (Deane J).
41   *Carter v Managing Partner Northmore Hale Davy & Leake* (1995) 183 CLR 121, 133 (Deane J).
42   *Carter v Managing Partner Northmore Hale Davy & Leake* (1995) 183 CLR 121, 161 (McHugh J).
43   *Grant v Downs* (1976) 135 CLR 674, 685 (Stephen, Mason, and Murphy JJ).
44   *R v Bell; Ex Parte Lees* (1980) 146 CLR 141, 152 (Stephen J).

In *Baker v Campbell*,[45] Justice Murphy said that CLP is

> essential for the orderly and dignified conduct of individual affairs in a social atmosphere which is being poisoned by official and unofficial eavesdropping and other invasions of privacy. The individual should be able to seek and obtain legal advice and legal assistance for innocent purposes, without the fear that what has been prepared... may be search or seized.[46]

Prior to that case, he had argued in dissent that

> The important public policy which justifies the privilege would often be defeated if the privilege were not generally available.[47]

While he did not expressly define the public policy underlying CLP, Murphy J implied that CLP may be more than a tool to optimise the efficiency of the courts and that it enabled the protection of other essential human rights.

In referring to the utilitarian argument for CLP, Justice Wilson said that the public interest underlying CLP was that lawyers were needed to enable the proper functioning of the courts.[48] Lawyers were necessary because of both complexity of law,[49] and the complex

> demands which the modern state makes upon its citizens... The adequate protection according to law of the privacy and liberty of the individual is an essential mark of a free society.[50]

Gummow J observed that CLP was 'a rule of law, the best explanation of which is that it affords a practical guarantee of fundamental rights.'[51] His

---

45   *Baker v Campbell* (1983) 153 CLR 52.
46   Ibid, 89 (Murphy J).
47   *O'Reilly v State Bank of Victoria Commissioners* (1983) 153 CLR 1, 27 (Murphy J).
48   *Baker v Campbell* (1983) 153 CLR 52, 93 – 94 (Wilson J).
49   Ibid, 94.
50   Ibid, 95 (Wilson J).
51   *Goldberg v Ng* (1995) 185 CLR 83, 121 (Gummow J).

Honour also said that the privilege

> protects the strong as well as the vulnerable, the shabby and dis-
> credited as well as the upright and virtuous, those whose cause is
> in public disfavour as much as those whose cause is held in pop-
> ular esteem.[52]

In the same case, Kirby J opined that CLP is

> essential to the defence of rights and freedoms and for the protec-
> tion of the individual... in legal difficulties. It is true that, some-
> times, hiding behind the privilege, are powerful wrong-doers. But
> the law protects them because the privilege is deeply embedded in
> our society's notions as to how the rule of law can best be achieved
> for all. The privilege protects the weak, the frightened, the unpop-
> ular and the disadvantaged.[53]

Justice Toohey stated that CLP is 'of fundamental importance to the protection and preservation of the rights, dignity, and equality of the ordinary citizen under the law.'[54]

The judicial comments from the High Court set out above may be divided into two categories – firstly, arguments that CLP protects a citizen
from the state by enforcing their rights,[55] and secondly, that because the
modern legal system is bewilderingly complex, individual citizens, especially the 'weak and uninformed,'[56] need legal help to navigate their
way through the legal system. Both arguments support CLP. CLP assists individual citizens in making use of their rights – against both the
state and others. Certainly many citizens would be ignorant of their legal rights without a lawyer's help, but must then ask why or how CLP is

---

52   *Commissioner, Australian Federal Police v Propend Finance Pty Ltd* (1997) 188 CLR
     501, 565 (Gummow J).

53   Ibid, 587 (Kirby J)

54   *Carter v Managing Partner Northmore Hale Davy & Leake* (1995) 183 CLR 121, 145
     (Toohey J).

55   E.g., the judgments of Deane, Toulson, Toohey, Kirby, and Gummow JJ.

56   E.g., the judgments of Wilson, Murphy, and Stephen JJ.

necessary to enable people to exercise their rights.

A fundamental aspect of the rule of law is that the laws must be know-able.[57] Every citizen should be able to learn and understand the laws to which they are subject or have access to someone who can explain them. Access to the law gives a citizen legal understanding so that they can make well-informed decisions. When the law is simple, it is easier for people to ascertain their rights under the laws that apply to them. Conversely, when citizens cannot read or access the law, then even a simple legal system does not help them know their rights unless they have access to someone who can explain them. Without such access or knowledge, the individual is left exposed to abuse by those in authority. In the 21st century, the complexity of law and society means that few of those without a legal education are able to know and enforce their rights, placing them in an unequal position before those in authority. Thus, to enforce their rights in a complex society, citizens require assis-tance from someone trained in law. Access to a lawyer thus enables and empowers individuals to they are more confident when there is a need to wisely resist the unreasonable pressure which is sometimes exercised by those in authority. Essentially, access to a lawyer places citizens who are not legally educated in the position of someone with full agency who is able to know, enforce, and rely upon their legal rights.

If we accept that equality of citizens is a significant purpose of CLP, it must then be asked whether the communication between a lawyer and client should be kept confidential. CLP enables a person to stand on the same ground as someone who is aware of their rights, by giving the per-son full access to their rights, liabilities, and legal options within a given situation. Therefore, if we are to equalise citizens before the state, the 'ignorant' must receive protection to prevent revelation of their legal ad-

---

57   See Encyclopedia Britannica, *Britannica Academic* (at 11 September 2018) 'Rule of Law,' or A V Dicey's classic statement of the principle, especially in A V Dicey, *Introduction to the Study of the Law of the Constitution* (MacMillan and Co, 3rd ed, 1889) 189.

vice, since those who are already aware of their rights do not need to disclose their circumstances before they make informed decisions. Therefore if a lawyer was forced to disclose advice given to a client who was uncertain about the law, the inequality between the legally educated and the uninformed, would be increased and the benefits of law would 'become the preserve of the few.'[58] In that light, CLP places both groups on a more equal footing. the otherwise uninformed client would have the option to waive CLP, and the legally informed person who did not require legal advice could 'make a clean breast of it.'[59] Again, if CLP did not make legal advice and communication confidential, then a person unaware of the law relevant to her case could still make informed choices about her options under the law. But the discussions and process by which she became informed of her rights would be subject to revelation and consideration by third parties. This would reduce social justice in society because it would increase the divide between those who are educated about the law and those who are not.

Thus one rationale underlying the High Court judgments noted above is that CLP operates to level the playing field between those who know the law and those who do not. This is a fundamental requirement of the rule of law and means that CLP serves as a 'bulwark against tyranny'.[60] CLP protects against tyranny because it lessens the risk that executive decisions will be made against them because they do not know how to defend themselves within the law. CLP thus empowers less knowledgeable members of society so that they can respond to appropriately to government control as the rule of law requires and assumes. Because CLP aids access to justice, it facilitates the administration of justice by enhancing societal confidence in the delivery of social justice.

58   Adrian Zuckerman, et al, *Zuckerman on Australian Civil Procedure* (LexisNexis Butterworths, 2018), 666.

59   *Anderson v Bank of British Columbia* (1876) 2 Ch D 644, 649 (Jessel MR)

60   *Attorney-General (NT) v Maurice* (1986) 161 CLR 475, 490 (Deane J).

V   A Human Right

The United Nations has stated in its *General Comments* that CLP is an in-trinsic part of the right to a fair trial.[61] This assertion recognises that hu-man rights are interconnected and rely on legal representation for their effective enforcement.[62] The interconnectedness of individual human rights is manifest in the fact that, for example, freedom of conscience is meaningless if one does not also have the freedom to express one's be-liefs. Furthermore, both of these rights are antecedent to any meaningful exercise of a right to freedom of association.

Similarly, the right to a fair trial and the right to freedom from arbitrary detention cannot be exercised without legal representation and legal representation is stunted if a lawyer and a client cannot communicate freely in the knowledge that neither will be forced to disclose that com-munication.[63] CLP is thus an essential part of the right to a fair trial. It ensures that a person can receive sound legal advice and be aware of the applicable law and of personal rights. Since CLP gives effect to a person's rights by enabling them to be known and enforced, CLP therefore enables the enforcement of one's human rights. CLP enables people. Whether CLP is identified as a component part of the right to legal representation or as a separate human right does not make a great difference in practice because the rights to legal representation is meaningless without CLP.

The relevance of the international law to Australia's use of CLP is mixed. While Australia has ratified but not domesticated the *International Cov-enant on Civil and Political Rights* (ICCPR), Australia has taken steps to

---

61   UNHRC, *General Comment No. 32: Article 14 Right to Equality before Courts and Tribunals and to a Fair Trial*, 90th sess, 9 July – 27 July 2007, UN DOC CCPR/C/GC/32 (2007), art 2 – 3.

62   See the discussion in Daniel J Whelan, *Indivisible Human Rights: A History* (University of Pennsylvania Press, 2011), 1 – 10. Note that Whelan criticises some of the language with rights, but the book's central paper revolves, among other things, around the conception of human rights as indivisible.

63   See UNHRC, *General Comment No. 32: Article 14 Right to Equality before Courts and Tribunals and to a Fair Trial*, 90th sess, 9 July – 27 July 2007, UN DOC CCPR/C/GC/32 (2007), art 2 – 3.

ensure human rights are considered in regards to evidence law and the passing of new bills. For example, s 134 of the *Evidence Act 1995* (NSW) (and other jurisdictions) requires that a judge, when deciding whether to admit illegally obtained evidence, must have regard to any right in the *ICCPR* that was breached in obtaining the evidence. Furthermore, under the *Human Rights (Parliamentary Scrutiny) Act 2011* (Cth), all new Bills put before the federal parliament must assess the impact on human rights and freedoms within Australia. However, as was argued in the *Roach* case, Australian law does not accept the authority of international law unless directed by a legislative provision, such as s 134 of the *Evidence Act 1995* (NSW).[64] Despite this fact, it has been noted that Australian courts may take note of international law,[65] and the legislative requirements to have regard to international law under the *Evidence Act 1995* (NSW) and *Human Rights (Parliamentary Scrutiny) Act 2011* (Cth) mean that the ongoing development of the principle of CLP as a human right is something which Australian legislators and courts may note when questions of CLP and its effects on other human rights arise.

VI   Defending Client Legal Privilege

If we do not understand these justifications for CLP, we are apt to think as Bentham argued, that CLP does no more than assist a guilty person to escape justice by allowing a lawyer to refuse to give evidence about his client. Refusing to admit such evidence must be justified convincingly if CLP is to be defended in parliament. The burden of Bentham's critique must be answered directly – does preventing a lawyer from giving evidence assist everyone before a court, or does it only aid someone who would otherwise face legal penalties? Even when it is argued that the courts do not work in a perfect environment and that CLP is needed to ensure a fair trial, we must be able to explain *why* CLP assists in ensuring

---

64   *Roach v Electoral Commissioner* (2007) 233 CLR 162, 224-225 [181] (Heydon J dissenting)

65   *Minister for Immigration and Multicultural and Indigenous Affairs v B* (2004) 219 CLR 365, 426 [171] (Kirby J).

a fair trial, and *why* a rule that prevents the admission of evidence aids the administration of justice more than allowing a court to receive that evidence.

Bentham argued that justice and trials are not games, and that legal rules should not be available to enable the guilty to avoid punishment.[66] Bentham did not accept the existence of human rights in the first place and so would have regarded the claim that CLP enabled the protection of rights as just one more example of a legal rule that could allow a guilty person to escape. However, Bentham's 'game' argument focussed only on one benefit of CLP that he saw accruing to guilty people. However, protecting the human rights of everyone, including those disadvantaged because of their lack of legal understanding, is not just about giving a guilty person a chance to escape a criminal charge. In many respects, that criticism of CLP is a caricature because it ignores the virtue of CLP in enabling ever member of society to achieve equality before the law. Bentham's criticism does not merely discount CLP's contribution to social justice in human society; it ignores it completely. For if CLP enables everyone to know and enforce their rights, then CLP is not really about assisting guilty people to escape justice; it has always been about enabling access to justice. In this light, as a rule of evidentiary exclusion, CLP is not just a rule of a game, but rather a law vested in sound public policy that identifies communications should remain confidential to ensure that all citizens can achieve equality before the law. The foundation of CLP then is not about assisting person to escape justice, but it is a practical measure focused on the accomplishment of fairness and social justice in any human society. CLP helps courts achieve justice because it contributes to ensuring all the parties to any suit have access to the legal knowledge they will need to prosecute their case effectively.

Bentham famously criticised the concept of natural rights as 'nonsense on stilts.'[67] Instead, Bentham argued that the 'substantive right is the

---

66   Bentham, (n 14), 316 – 317.
67   Jeremy Bentham, *Rights, Representation, and Reform: Nonsense on Stilts and Other Writ-*

child of law.'[68] In other words, the only real rights are rights created and protected by law, even though each right created also infringes upon a person's liberty by creating obligations upon that person to respect other persons' rights. Bentham was concerned that the creation or recognition of any right derogated from liberty, because each right also created a correlative obligation.[69] Nevertheless, he recognised the office of states was to protect citizens from suffering,[70] and that states needed to create substantive rights to personal security and property to protect citizens even though the rights created did infringe upon and limit the liberty of other members of society.[71]

However, human rights are now recognised in international law as the inherent rights of all human beings,[72] though they are only effective to the extent that individual states recognise, enforce or protect them. Human rights laws protect human beings from suffering and provide personal security. In other words, most modern human rights protect the human needs which Bentham agreed that states should protect. When CLP is seen as enabling human equality, it forms part of the set of rights (such as the right to a fair trial) that enforce and protect other rights. Thus, even if one were to agree with Bentham that natural rights are 'nonsense on stilts', one can still accept that CLP contributes to a just society and does not exist to enable a legal game that allows some guilty persons to escape justice. Properly understood, CLP is essential to the continued meaning and operation of all other legal rights, since they would not be enforceable without it, and therefore a right which states should legislate to give it substantive effect

---

ings on the French Revolution (P Schofield, C Pease-Watkin, and C Blamires, eds, Oxford University Press, first published 1816, 2002 ed), 330.

68   Ibid, 398.

69   Philip Schofield, 'Jeremy Bentham's Nonsense on Stilts' (2003) 15(1) *Utilitas* 1, 17.

70   Jeremy Bentham, 'Principles of the Civil Code' in *The Collected Works of Jeremy Bentham* (ed John Bowring, Russell & Russell, first published 1832, 1962 ed), 302

71   Ibid, 301 – 302.

72   See the preamble to *Universal Declaration of Human Rights*, GA Res 217A (III), UN GAOR, UN Doc A/810 (10 December 1948), which acknowledges that inherent dignity and rights are the foundation of freedom.

Bentham argued that, in order to give justice according to law, a court must have all the relevant evidence. All relevant evidence was required to 'punish the guilty' and render a just verdict between two disputing parties based on the circumstances of each case.[73] That lofty goal suggests that relevant evidence should not be lightly excluded from any court hearing.[74] Nevertheless, there are limits to the steps a court should take to achieve justice. Ironically, Bentham did not support removing religious confession privilege because that would effectively ban Catholicism without good enough reason: 'In compensation for the evil of this tyranny [banning Catholicism], no good would in any shape be produced.'[75] And as Bruce LJ famously stated, 'Truth, like all other good things, may be loved unwisely – may be pursued too keenly – may cost too much.'[76]

International human rights instruments make it clear that there should be limits to the pursuit of truth, by forbidding the use of torture or other coercion to obtain evidence.[77] The recognition of the right to a fair trial and other protections of the accused provided in international human rights instruments suggest that courts should be not concerned with truth at all costs, but must protect the dignity of the person, including the dignity of an accused.[78] CLP balances the protection of the dignity of the human person against a court's need for all the evidence in the pursuit of truth.[79] Instead of leaving the realisation of all human rights up to individual judges, the predetermined recognition of CLP as a human right ensures the needed balance is possible. Although individual ques-

---

73   Bentham, (n 14), 303 – 310.

74   Ibid, 303.

75   Jeremy Bentham, *An Introductory View of the Rationale of Evidence; For the Use of Non-Lawyers as well as Lawyers* in *The Works of Jeremy Bentham* (Hunt & Clarke, first published 1843, 1995 edition) ,vol 6, 99.

76   *Pearse v Pearse* (1846) 63 ER 950, 957 – 958.

77   See *International Covenant on Civil and Political Rights*, opened for signature 16 December 1966, 999 UNTS 171 (entered into force 23 March 1976), art 7, against cruel and inhuman treatment or torture.

78   See, e.g., ibid, art 14.

79   *Waterford v Commonwealth* (1987) 163 CLR 54, 64 (Mason and Wilson JJ).

tions about CLP are necessarily left to judges, the legal recognition of this privilege as a human right provides a policy foundation that frames the judicial evaluation of questions about it in individual cases. If CLP is recognised as essential to equality before the law by placing a less legally educated person in the position of someone who knows the law, then it is less difficult to explain why the confidentiality of those communications should be protected. For if that confidentiality is not preserved, inequality returns. The dignity of the human person is therefore enhanced by CLP.

The denial of CLP because of Bentham's contrary argument for equality before the law, would, ironically, *remove* equality before the law. Bentham argued that CLP was a rule to set lawyers above other professions, since judges (former lawyers) make the law and therefore give special treatment to other lawyers. However, if one differentiates between those who know and understand their rights because of legal education and those who do not, then the denial of CLP becomes a surrogate for the denial of substantive justice to those who do not know the law. Where CLP is denied to citizens who do not know the law, they will be practically unable to understand and enforce their legal rights. CLP is required to achieve equality between all citizens. This is reinforced in international rights law, where each person has a right to legal counsel of their own choice.[80]

This analysis confirms that CLP protects other human rights. Law exists, at least in part, to enable each human person to enforce her rights under law;[81] 'to render each [person her] due'[82] and prevent abuses of power by those in authority.[83] CLP protects and facilitates human rights by enabling every person accused of crime to know their rights, and to

---

80   *International Covenant on Civil and Political Rights*, opened for signature 16 December 1966, 999 UNTS 171 (entered into force 23 March 1976), art 14(3)(b) and (d).

81   Adrian Zuckerman, *Zuckerman on Civil Procedure* (Sweet & Maxwell, 3rd ed, 2013), 813 [16.10].

82   Justinian, (n 5), 1 [trans of: *Institutiones*, I.1].

83   Zuckerman, (n 81), 813 [16.10].

be able to enforce them. CLP thus plays a vital role in enabling the law to achieve its goals. While enforcing confidentiality seemed like an extreme measure to Jeremy Bentham since it limited the evidence available to a court, properly understood CLP ensures full equality of different persons before the law. CLP is thus a worthwhile limitation on the pursuit of truth.

VII   Conclusion

This paper has argued that the best justification for CLP within Australian jurisprudence is that it enables people to know their rights so that the law cannot be misused against them. Because the modern legal system is complicated, CLP continues to allow human individuals completely confidential communication with their chosen lawyers in the long-term interests of equality.

This answers Bentham's criticism powerful one-liner, that CLP only helps the guilty. It answers Bentham's criticism because it explains that law is not just about delivering criminal justice. It is also about enabling the equality of all human beings and the accessibility of the full spectrum of human rights. If a person could not obtain legal advice, she would be ignorant of the protections available to her in the law and, she would be unable to defend herself against those with more knowledge of the law including the state. Any abrogation of CLP thus contributes to social inequality. As a number of Australian High Court judges have said, CLP serves the administration of justice by giving effect to a person's legal and human rights.

CLP also underpins, preserves and enables human rights. CLP gives effect to human rights by ensuring that when human individuals are brought to any trial, they can so that the representation guaranteed to them under international human rights instruments can be provided can be provided to them with full understanding of all the nuances of their case.

A better understanding of the reasons why CLP remains important will enable Australian parliaments to make wise legislative decisions when it is proposed that CLP be further abrogated in the interests of temporary evidential expediency in future cases. Better understanding of CLP will also help judges and lawyers defend CLP when it is challenged in court and in the public sphere in the future.

Bibliography

A   *Articles/Books/Reports*

Auburn, Jonathan, *Legal Professional Privilege: Law & Theory* (Hart Publishing, 2003)

Australian Law Reform Commission, *Privilege in Perspective: Client Legal Privilege in Federal Investigations*, Report No 107 (2007)

Australian Law Reform Commission, *Traditional Rights and Freedoms – Encroachments by Commonwealth Laws*, Report No 129 (2016)

Australian Law Reform Commission, *Uniform Evidence Law*, Report No 102 (2006)

Bentham, Jeremy, *Rights, Representation, and Reform: Nonsense on Stilts and Other Writings on the French Revolution* (P Schofield, C Pease-Watkin, and C Blamires, eds, Oxford University Press, first published 1815, 2002 ed)

Bentham, Jeremy, *An Introductory View of the Rationale of Evidence; For the Use of Non-Lawyers as well as Lawyers* in *The Works of Jeremy Bentham* (Hunt & Clarke, first published 1843, 1995 ed)

Bentham, Jeremy 'Principles of the Civil Code' in *The Collected Works of Jeremy Bentham* (ed John Bowring, Russell & Russell, first published 1832, 1962 ed)

Bentham, Jeremy, *Rationale of Judicial Evidence* (Hunt and Clarke, first published 1827, 1995 ed)

Desiatnik, Ronald J, *Legal Professional Privilege in Australia* (LexisNexis Butterworths, 3rd ed, 2017)

Dicey, A V, *Introduction to the Study of the Law of the Constitution* (MacMillan and Co, 3rd ed, 1889)

Encyclopedia Britannica, *Britannica Academic* (at 11 September 2018) 'Rule of Law'

Heydon, J D, *Cross on Evidence* (LexisNexis Butterworths, 9th ed, 2013)

Ho, H L, 'Legal Professional Privilege and the Integrity of Legal Representation' (2015) 9(2) *Legal Ethics* 163

Justinian, *The Institutes of Justinian* (J T Abdy trans, Cambridge University Press, 1876) [trans of: *Institutiones*]

McNicol, Suzanne B, *The Law of Privilege* (LawBook Co, 1992)

Radin, Max, 'The Privilege of Confidential Communication Between Lawyer and Client' (1928) 16(6) *California Law Review* 487

Schofield, Philip, 'Jeremy Bentham's Nonsense on Stilts' (2003) 15(1) *Utilitas* 1

Tsalanidis, Joseph, *Legal Professional Privilege: Its Rationale and Exceptions* (LLM thesis, The University of Melbourne, 1984)

Whelan, Daniel J, *Indivisible Human Rights: A History* (University of Pennsylvania Press, 2011)

Wigmore, J H, *Evidence in Trials at Common Law* (Little, Brown, & Co., McNaughton rev ed, 1961)

Zuckerman, A A S, 'Legal Professional Privilege – The Cost of Absolutism' (1996) 112 *Law Quarterly Review* 535

Zuckerman, Adrian, *Zuckerman on Civil Procedure* (Sweet & Maxwell, 3rd ed, 2013)

Zuckerman, Adrian, Stefanie Wilkins, Jonathan Adamopoulos, Andrew Higgins, Stephanie Hooper, and Alexander Vial, *Zuckerman on Australian Civil Procedure* (LexisNexis Butterworths, 2018)

B   *Cases*

Anderson v Bank of British Columbia (1876) 2 Ch D 644

Attorney-General (NT) v Maurice (1986) 161 CLR 475

Baker v Campbell (1983) 153 CLR 52

Carter v Managing Partner, Northmore Hale Davy & Leake (1995) 183 CLR 121

Commissioner, Australian Federal Police v Propend Finance Pty Ltd (1997) 199 CLR 501

D v NSPCC [1978] AC 171

Daniels Corporation v Australian Competition and Consumer Commission (2002) 213 CLR 543

Esso Australia Resources Ltd v Commissioner of Taxation (Cth) (1999) 201 CLR 49

Goldberg v Ng (1995) 185 CLR 83

Minister for Immigration and Multicultural and Indigenous Affairs v B (2004) 219 CLR 365

O'Reilly v State Bank of Victoria Commissioners (1983) 153 CLR 1

Pearse v Pearse (1846) 63 ER 950

R v Bell; Ex Parte Lees (1980) 146 CLR 141

Roach v Electoral Commissioner (2007) 233 CLR 162

Waterford v The Commonwealth (1987) 163 CLR 54

C   *Legislation*

Evidence Act 1995 (Cth)

Evidence Act 1995 (NSW)

Evidence Act 2008 (Vic)

Evidence Act 2001 (Tas)

Human Rights (Parliamentary Scrutiny) Act 2011 (Cth)

D   *Treaties & International Instruments*

Basic Principles on the Role of Lawyers, Eighth UN Congress on the Prevention of Crime and Treatment of Offenders, 27 August – 7 September 1990, UN Doc A/Conf.133/28/Rev.1 (1991)

Convention for the Protection of Human Rights and Fundamental Freedoms, opened for signature 27 May 2009, CETS No 204 (entered into force 1 September 2009)

International Covenant on Civil and Political Rights, opened for signature 16 December 1966, 999 UNTS 171 (entered into force 23 March 1976)

UNHRC, *General Comment No 32: Article 14 Right to Equality before Courts and Tribunals and to a Fair Trial*, 90th sess, 9 July – 27 July 2007, UN DOC CCPR/C/GC/32 (2007)

2

Where the Pell Judgment Went Fatally Wrong

John Finnis

This article is reprinted with the author's permission following initial publication by 'Quadrant' online on September 9, 2019. It has not been through the double-blind peer review process to which the other articles in this book have been subject.

Anyone tempted to believe George Pell did what he was convicted of doing should read first the majority judgment of the Court of Appeal majority ("Judgment"), next the fuller transcript of the complainant's allegations that is given in paras. 415-55 of the dissenting judgment ("Dissent"), and then the Wikipedia account (with numerous links) of Operation Midland.

If you take this short tour, you will see the Judgment fall apart under your eyes. The Judgment's sequencing (Falsity, Improbability, Impossibility) reverses the rational order of treatment. Its handling of Archbishop Pell's alibi defence concludes abruptly in para. 143 by placing the onus of proof exactly where the law quoted in para. 142 says it cannot be: on the defence. Its construction of a five or six minute window of opportunity for the Archbishop to commit singularly vile offences against two thirteen-year-old boys, in the Priests' Sacristy, has a similar incoherence thinly veiled behind an 'of course' and an evasive 'taking the evidence as a whole'.

A brief account of those three ways the 352-paragraph Judgment goes wrong will indicate how the jury's one-word verdicts could be as wrong as one should conclude they were.

Of course, there is another secure route to that conclusion: read the Dissent. It brings to light many other reasons to reject the complainant's allegations. But it is long and winding. Here, then, is one shorter route.

One: Rational sequencing reversed

The Judgment went wrong by considering first the defence's contention that the complainant's tales of rapes and other assaults by the Archbishop of Melbourne were false, along with the defence's alternative explanations of that falsity: dishonest fabrication or honest fantasy (or some combination of these). The defence had no obligation to suggest, and did not begin to suggest, any *motive* for fabricating or any *cause* for fantasising. On the defence case, the falsity of the allegations is a *conclusion from all the evidence* taken together: that is, from the gaps and alterations in the allegations, from their inherent improbability, and from their incompatibility with the wealth of evidence that the Archbishop was absent from the sacristies at the relevant times (impossibility) and that, in all probability, numerous other people were coming and going and/or unrobing and/or sitting about in the Priests' Sacristy at those times (impossibility or improbability).

By treating falsity as a distinct argument (rather than a conclusion from other arguments) – and also by treating it *before* improbability and impossibility – the Judgment displays deep confusion about the case's basic logic, aborts its own rational consideration of the defence, and effectively reverses the onus of proof. The defence had presented [60] the three matters in a rational and cumulatively inter-connected sequence: (A) the testimony's improbability both inherently and as given with inconsistencies, opportunistic embellishments, and sheer mistakes, (B) its impossibility as demonstrated by much counter-evidence, and (C) the appropriate conclusions: the testimony, however 'compelling' as delivered [59], [87], [90], is certainly false, or most probably false, and, at any rate, the possibility of its falsity is so real that the jury should have doubted it, and Pell in both law and justice should have been acquitted.   But the Judgment [64], in reversing the sequence, also practically eliminated the inter-connections and cumulation, that is, the rational bearing of (B) on (A), and of (A) and (B) together on (C). And it made this reversal for no stated reason, but just as something 'it is convenient' to do [64].

Under 'falsity', thus misconceived, the Judgment dealt with a knot of issues that could indeed be rightly considered – but only *provisionally* considered – *before* considering the evidence about the Archbishop's absence (impossibility) and other people's presence (improbability or impossibility). This is the knot of issues about the internal (im)plausibility and (in)coherence of the complainant's testimony and the (in)consistency of his several iterations of it. Watching twice (like the jury) the video of two of those iterations, the Judgment's authors found him *credible and true.*

The phrase is not theirs but sums up the conclusions reached and opinions conveyed in this part of the Judgment. 'Credible and true' is the phrase actually used by the very senior officer of the Metropolitan Police's Operation Midland to describe the detailed testimony given to multiple police officers on multiple occasions by 'Nick' (one Carl Beech), presenting himself as a victim/survivor and/or witness of sexual abuse, and sex-murders, witnessed by him from 1975 (aged 7) to 1984 (aged 16), at the hands of a former prime minister, former Heads of MI5 and MI6, a former Home Secretary, a former Chief of the Defence Staff, and other named persons of similar standing in British public life. In early 2015, the same year the Victorian complainant came forward to testify to Victorian Police that he was a victim/survivor of Archbishop Pell, those of the British persons just mentioned still living had their lives irreparably damaged by 20-hour police searches and public police accusations all made in total reliance on 'Nick's' testimony. And in 2019, while the Court of Appeal was hearing Cardinal Pell's appeal and writing the Judgment, Carl Beech, long called by the police and media a 'victim/survivor', was being tried (over ten weeks) and in due course sentenced to 18 years imprisonment for perverting the course of justice. For despite Beech's ability to describe places where these public figures were likely to have been, there turned out to be no truth in his accusations – though, while sufficiently insulated from counter-evidence and accurate contextualisation, they had been judged by experienced police detectives to be truthful and 'credible *and true*'.

The Pell Judgment declares its authors' entire satisfaction with the truthfulness and accuracy of the complainant, and it does so *before* turning to confront any of the contextualising counter-evidence. The effect, despite its routine preliminary affirmations that the defence has no onus [65] (also [129]), is clear: to place on the defence the burden of proving the testimony false, the onus, that is to say, of (in one of the Judgment's several erroneous formulations) 'establishing the certainty which the [defence's] argument of impossibility asserted' [131]. That indefensible reversal is the topic of sec. two below.

Meanwhile, the Judgment finds that the credibility of the complainant's testimony was 'considerably enhanced by the accuracy of his description' of the sacristy in which he said he was raped etc.[95], and by the fact, 'more striking still', that because of redecorating works, the Archbishop was, unusually, having to robe and disrobe in that sacristy – the Priests' Sacristy – rather than in the adjoining one reserved to his use [96]. These two facts were [97]:

> independent confirmation of A's account of having been in the

Priests' Sacristy in that period. There was nothing to suggest that his knowledge of those matters could have been obtained otherwise. A's evidence was that he had never been in the Priests' Sacristy before.

These bits of 'independent confirmation' (what used to be called corroboration) each fall apart.

As to the first: the Judgment promptly contradicts both its own 'nothing to suggest' claim and its claim about 'A's evidence'. For under cross examination, A accepted [97] ([429], [836], [909]-[910]) that he had been given a cathedral tour, on becoming a choir boy, and accepted that such a tour would have included (though he said he could not recollect this) a visit to the Priests' Sacristy.

As to the second fact: the complainant's testimony in no way suggested that Pell had entered to disrobe; it just said [44] ([432]) he entered, 'planted himself in the doorway' (the doors of the sacristy from the corridor leading back to the sanctuary, aisles and nave) and challenged the boys. Moreover, there was a period of months in which the Archbishop was obliged to use the Priests' Sacristy for robing and disrobing [347], and nothing to suggest that at other times he was never to be seen in the Priests' Sacristy heading to or from his own adjacent sacristy (further from the cathedral's liturgical activity) via the door in the partition-wall between the sacristies, or conversing in either sacristy with priests or altar servers [263]. And the complainant as a choirboy must have gone right past the main door of the Priests' Sacristy (not to mention the main door of the Archbishop's Sacristy) on many occasions, at times when it was likely to be open before or after services.

The reluctantly admitted preliminary choir tour weakens to the point of extinguishing the corroboration which the Judgment finds in the complainant's knowledge (such as it was) of sacristy layout. But even setting aside the tour, nothing suggested that – at any time while he was a choirboy – he might not have peeked or ducked into the Priests' Sacristy and seen its arrangement, in an escapade, perhaps of seconds, perhaps even of minutes, perhaps accompanied or alone, just conceivably even for wine-swigging, an escapade that included no confrontation with any Archbishop (or with anyone) and no oral rape. The 'independent confirmation' gets nowhere near tending to confirm any claims concerning the Archbishop.

About those claims, and the question of 'independent support' for them, the Dissent rightly summarises the position:

> 'There was no forensic, or other objective evidence, to support [the complainant's] account'; indeed, 'the jury were invited to accept his evidence without there being any independent evidence to support it' [410], '...entirely unsupported...', 'no supporting evidence of any kind' [412], [925], [1104].

And the Judgment, while clutching at straws to find confirmation, passingly admits the falsity of the complainant's denials that he had ever been in the Priests' Sacristy before or after the day on which, he said, he and another boy (now dead) swigged wine and were raped there. The Judgment reports and ignores this admission as blandly as it ignores the evidence [827]-[831] that his testimony about the colour of the wine and of its bottle was all untrue, and that both his description and his recollection of the relevant part of the sacristy, so far from being impressively accurate, were quite inaccurate [834]-[835].

Two: Onus of proof reversed

The shortest of all routes to discovering that the Judgment has gone catastrophically wrong is to read paras. 139 to 143 and para. 151. Para. 139 summarises one of the ways in which the defence argued that the alleged offending in the Priests' Sacristy was impossible: Archbishop Pell was at the relevant time far away at the west door with his master of ceremonies, Fr. Portelli, meeting and greeting worshippers. Portelli's testimony (not to mention the testimony of many other witnesses) was cogent evidence of that, and if true constituted an alibi for Cardinal Pell.

In para. 140, the Judgment remarks that the concepts of alibi, impossibility and (lack of) opportunity are 'of course, closely inter-connected.' But it goes on to say that the defence at the trial had (at least in its closing) avoided the word 'alibi', had asked the trial judge not to use it, and [141] had not asked for a direction to the jury in the form appropriate to alibi defences. Without making any comment on those features of the conduct of the defence at the trial, or on the fact that the prosecution in its final trial address [241] had called some of the evidence 'alibi', the Judgment then and there [142] sets out the law applicable to alibi defences. Neither here nor anywhere else did the Judgment suggest that the defence of George Pell is disqualified from relying on this law.

To state it, the Judgment uses a source different from the Dissent's sources [396], [625], [628], [949] but with precisely the same legal content. The jury cannot rightly convict unless *the prosecution has 'remove[d] or eliminate[d] any reasonable possibility'* that the accused was not at the alleged crime-scene (the sacristy) but somewhere else instead (the west door).

Then, with a startling lurch, the Judgment goes straight from stating that law to stating [143] its own position, essentially its fundamental conclusion about the whole case:

> Having read all of the opportunity evidence and watched some of it, we are not persuaded that the evidence of any individual witness, or the evidence taken as a whole, established impossibility in the sense contended for by the defence.

The next sentence adds: 'In pt II of the reasons, we explain that conclusion by reference to the evidence relied on in support of each of the individual impossibility contentions.' To wrap up part I, its main part, the Judgment proceeds to give an example [144]-[147] of its way of dealing with an 'individual impossibility contention', and then circles back to the general significance of the impossibility v. possibility argument. The substance of para. 143's astonishing transfer of the burden of proof to the defence is now repeated [151]:

> As we have said, the onus of proof required the prosecution to defeat [the argument of impossibility]. It was both necessary and sufficient for that purpose to persuade the jury that the events were not impossible and that there was a realistic opportunity for the offending to occur.

Finally, in relation to 'opportunity' (the remaining facet of the alibi – impossibility – no opportunity complex), para. 170 repeats that the *prosecution* need do no more than establish a 'realistic opportunity'. What had emerged, says para. 170, was 'not a catalogue of "impossibilities"... bnterfainties and possibilities.... Plainly enough, uncertainty multiplied upon uncertainty does not – cannot – *demonstrate impossibility.*'

Now it is significant that some of these 'uncertainties' were rustled up out of witnesses' syntax and, like other 'uncertainties', were in any syntax and on any view unchallenged near-certainties. But that is not the subject of this article. Here the point is that – as is laid down in the legal rule, quoted in para. 142 but then left hanging enigmatically in the air – it was not for the defence to 'demonstrate' or 'establish' impossibility. Nor was it sufficient for the prosecution to establish possibility in the strict sense of 'not impossible', or even to establish *realistic* possibility in the sense of 'realistically, or in reality, *not impossible*'. There is a wide chasm between, on the one hand, the Judgment's *there was a realistic possibility that the rapes could have happened* and, on the other hand, the law's standard, quoted without demur by the Judgment, a standard which demands a finding of not guilty unless there was *no realistic possibility that he was away from the sacristy* and additionally *no realistic possibility that at least one other person (concelebrating priest, altar server, sacristan) was in the sacristy or (parishioner) at its open door for even a moment in the five or six minutes after Mass on 15*

December 1996.

Three: Evidence wrongly assessed

Still, it would be grossly mistaken to think that this defendant was entitled to be acquitted only, or even mainly, because of some legal rule about alibi defences, a rule perhaps surprisingly demanding on the prosecution. The point of the preceding paragraphs was to show, as briefly as possible, how very unsatisfactory the Judgment is in discharging its primary responsibility to *apply the law coherently* to the case before the court.

To see why everyone should think that George Pell not only was legally entitled to be acquitted but simply *did not do* any of the criminal acts alleged, one may, once again, take the long route of reading the Dissent. Its conclusions are expressed with great restraint [1051]-[1111]; in substance: anyone reasonably considering the evidence should doubt – reasonably doubt – his guilt. Very illuminating is the abundant evidence the Dissent assembles, and the report it gives [1047] of the impression made upon this careful and experienced judge by watching on video many witnesses – both the complainant and a selected eleven of the many witnesses to practical impossibility, alibi and lack of opportunity. (Tellingly, the Judgment alludes to its authors' impressions on watching the complainant on video, but about other witnesses watched is silent.)

But besides that long Dissenting route, there is, again, a short traverse: a brief examination of a passage in which, not the Dissent, but the Judgment is handling the facts, just one of the many sets of facts on which it touches.

This particular passage [293]-[300] concerns the question whether there really could have been a period of five or six minutes, right after the conclusion of Mass, in which this archbishop could be alone in the Priests' Sacristy, having his way first with B (now deceased, having denied ever being interfered with), then with A, and then in another sordid way with A, uninterrupted by anyone (and after instructing A to 'undo his [A's] pants and take them right off' [47] so that the Archbishop could commit this third set of offences – and be yet more irretrievably exposed as a wicked criminal if anyone came in or even glanced in). To find the five or six minutes that, according to A, the offences against him and B took to complete, the Judgment deploys an 'of course'.

Now the Judgment had earlier used an 'of course' to somewhat similar effect [131]:

> It is, of course, of the very nature of an impossibility argument that it seeks to establish with sufficient certainty that the events could not have happened as alleged...

That 'of course' had the effect of muffling what was going on (as was shown in the last section): shifting to the defence the onus of '*establishing* [alibi/impossibility/lack of opportunity] with sufficient certainty', and in the process relieving the prosecution of *its* burden of disproving alibi, etc.

So too, with the 'of course' in para. 296 (here quoted in full, with emphases, exclamations and interpolations added):

> The effect of the servers' evidence was that the unlocking of the Sacristy door, and their bowing to the Crucifix [inside that Sacristy, to mark the end of their procession duties and the beginning of their altar duties], occurred soon after the procession [to the west door and then back, whether inside or outside, to the east end] finished and that, by the time they returned [from the Sacristy!] to the sanctuary to assist [the sacristan] Potter [in clearing the sanctuary], the door was already unlocked. [!] On that view, it was quite possible for the Sacristy to have been unlocked and unattended at around the time A said he and B broke away from the procession. The clearing of the sanctuary had, of course, to await the end of the private prayer for [= of] parishioners. The

Crown case as presented to the jury was that 'there is this hiatus, this gap' during which the first incident [oral rapes etc. over 5 to 6 minutes] had occurred.

And the Judgment committed itself to that Crown case [300]:

> taking the evidence as a whole, it was open to the jury to find that the assaults took place in the 5-6 minutes of private prayer time, and that this was before the 'hive of activity' described by the other [= other than Potter] witnesses began.

In framing its theory of guilt in this way, the Judgment was selecting one of two different accounts given by Potter. (He was testifying when aged about 84, about events over 20 years earlier, in 1996, when he had already been sacristan for nearly 35 years.). The Judgment silently ignores one of the accounts and relies on the other. But each is incompatible with the complainant's story.

On one account, reported by the Dissent in para. 504, Potter unlocked the Priests' Sacristy door *almost as soon* as the procession (with the choirboys including A and B near the front, followed by six to twelve altar servers, any priests, and at the end the Archbishop) set out from the sanctuary area, moving down the central nave to reach the west door. Other witnesses supported this timing explicitly [299] or implicitly [297], [298]. But it was not deployed by the prosecution or the Judgment. For although it entailed that the Sacristy was unlocked and might therefore, as a matter of physical possibility, be entered (as alleged by the complainant A) by errant choirboys and an even more errant Archbishop arriving on the scene after the procession had concluded or nearly concluded, it equally entailed that, at that same (alleged) time and at all times compatible with the accusations, the Sacristy was in constant use, first by the sacristan and then by both him and some or all of the altar servers.

So, instead, the prosecution and the Judgment rely upon sacristan Potter's other account. Summarised by the Dissent in para. 505, it is given by the Judgment in para. 293 like this:

> It was common ground that Potter was the person who unlocked the Priests' Sacristy [within which the alleged rapes etc. occurred on 15 December 1996] and that he did so after Mass. His evidence was that, after the choir and clergy had processed to the west door, he would go the sanctuary, where he would wait until parishioners had finished what he called their 'private time' for prayer after the service. This was typically a period of five or six minutes. He would then take books from the sanctuary and unlock the door to the Priests' Sacristy. He would then return to the sanctuary to gather up the sacred vessels and – sometimes with the assistance of the altar servers – would take them back to the Priests' Sacristy.

Thus the prosecution's and the Judgment's theory rests entirely on (i) accepting, 'of course', Potter's somewhat disputed evidence that sanctuary clearing (and the resultant traffic to and from the Priests' Sacristy) was delayed for five or six minutes after the end of Mass (to permit parishioners' private prayer), while simultaneously (ii) overlooking the necessary implications of another integral part of his same account, a part disputed by no other witness and stated without a qualm in para. 293, as we have just seen: during that '5-6 minutes hiatus for parishioners' prayer' the Priests' Sacristy door was locked.

So, part by part or 'taken as a whole', the evidence as summarised in the Judgment left no room at all for the Judgment's conclusion in [300]. Neither of Potter's accounts left time – still less the five or six minutes of solitude alleged by the complainant – for someone to commit offences against choirboys in the Priests' Sacristy. Potter's '5-6 minutes of prayer time' account affirmed, without challenge, that the Sacristy door was locked until the end of that time, and the *only* other evidence (Potter's and others') about the 'hive of activity' in that Sacristy was that it began much sooner than '5-6 minutes' after Mass.

The Judgment's conclusion, it is worth adding, is excluded also, and equally completely, by a plain fact unconsidered in the Judgment but obvious from all the evidence and the Judgment's map of the cathedral. 'A' said that his escapade with 'B' began when the procession had nearly ended. But by that time, the '5-6 minutes' prayer time allotted by the Judgment for the assaults had been used up.

Four: Summary

The Judgment's contention that the complainant's evidence was not false should only have been made by reference to the whole of the evidence, and not just by reference to his appearing credible. The contemporaneous case of Beech simply illustrates the point: accusations made by a complainant about sexual abuse who was very credible to many experienced officers were shown to have been entirely false.

Despite their recitations of the rules about onus, the majority shifted the onus onto the defence by saying that he had failed to establish that certain matters were improbable or (practically) impossible.

In satisfying themselves that there was a five- or six-minute window of opportunity – an unlocked and traffic-free door – the majority deployed a reference in the sacristan's evidence to 'five or six minutes'. They not only ignored other evidence from him and other witnesses that ferrying of stuff from sanctuary to sacristy would begin immediately the procession left the sanctuary – but also failed to see that any window of opportunity was eliminated by what they themselves were without demur recording as the sacristan's actual proposition: that during the whole 'five or six minutes' the sacristy door remained locked.

If the Judgment could go wrong in these ways, and not notice its own obvious errors, how much more so could the second jury.

3

The jury in its historical perspective

A. Keith Thompson

Introduction

In this chapter, I explain that the English jury is a completely different animal than it was when created between the 11th and the 13th centuries. And I reason, since the form of the jury was constantly changed between the 11th and the 16th centuries so that the monarch could better achieve justice as he saw it even though the underlying institution had become sacred, we should not be afraid to continue to tinker with it now as we also seek better justice.

In its original Norman form, the jury was an adaptation of an older Anglo-Saxon method that locals used to safely identify and catch dangerous criminals who no one individual was courageous enough to arrest and subject to trial. William the Conqueror simply adapted the idea that the same locals who identified Anglo-Saxon criminals could tell him who owned what so that he could collect taxes proportionate to wealth throughout his new dominion. Later William adapted that idea and held the same locals captive until they delivered the person or persons who had murdered his unpopular occupying troops or officials, or he fined those 'jurors' if culprits were not delivered.

The Conqueror's grandson Henry II experimented further with the delivery of justice a century later particularly in his *Constitutions of Clarendon* (1166). Not everyone was happy with his reforms to church jurisdiction, and his stoush with Archbishop Thomas Becket about the resulting double jeopardy of clergy led to Becket's murder in 1170. Henry II's changes also involved jury adaptations, but I am getting ahead of myself. The point is that from the time the Normans began using it, the jury was constantly adapted, and the idea that the aura of sanctity that came to surround it later renders it constitutionally beyond improvement, is unhistorical and unhelpful. Modern politicians ought to continue to discuss improvements. So by way of more detailed introduction, here is part of that story.

Three months after the Barons forced King John to sign the *Magna Carta* in June 1215 at Runnymede promising trial by peers,[1] Pope Innocent III issued a Papal Bull annulling it.[2] Three months after that in November 1215, the Pope convened the Fourth Lateran Council at the Lateran Palace in Rome and forbade clergy anywhere in the world to be involved in trials other than those convened by the Church.[3] Those two papal decisions caused considerable difficulty back in England. For though William Marshall as regent, voluntarily reinstated a slightly amended version of the *Magna Carta* to secure baronial support for the new nine year old King Henry III after King John died unexpectedly on 12 October 1216,[4] there was no obvious way to replace the clergy who had been an

---

1　　Article 39 of the original 1215 version of the *Magna Carta* reads:
　　　　No free man shall be seized or imprisoned, or stripped of his rights or possessions, or outlawed or exiled, or deprived of his standing in any way, nor will we proceed with force against him, or send others to do so, except by the lawful judgment of his equals or by the law of the land.
　　　While this provision did not guarantee trial by jury, the phrase, "lawful judgment of his equals" suggests the development of the jury by King Henry II (reigned 1154 to 1189) discussed below, was popular and becoming established as a credible mode of criminal trial (see for example, John H. Hatcher, "Magna Charta and the Jury System", *American Bar Association Journal* (1938) Volume 24, Issue 7, 555-558).

2　　Nicholas Vincent, *Magna Carta, A Very Short Introduction* (Oxford University Press, 2012) 75. The papal bull was dated 24 August 1215.

3　　Papal Encyclical's Online, February 20, 2017, "Fourth Lateran Council: 1215", < https://www.papalencyclicals.net/councils/ecum12-2.htm>.

4　　British Library, "William Marshal", *n.d.* <https://www.bl.uk/people/william-marshal>.

integral part of criminal trials in England in the past.

These were times of conflict and uncertain politics. King John had been excommunicated in 1209 by Pope Innocent III because he would not support the Pope's candidate as Archbishop of Canterbury.[5] But a compromise under which he accepted the Pope's appointment of Stephen Langton to that office, had been worked out in 1213 and the interdict which prevented English priests conducting religious services since 1208 had been lifted. The political power of the Pope was in crescendo. But conflict between kings and the popes in the twelfth and thirteenth centuries, was not confined to England. All over the continent Pope Innocent III was directing secular lords in the conduct of their kingdoms and punishing recalcitrants. The interdict imposed on the English Church between 1208 and 1213 was but one example of that punishment and enforcement of Church control. Two other examples came as instructions from the Lateran Council in 1215. The seal of confession became binding upon the entire church – no priest could disclose what he learned in confession anywhere on pain of excommunication, and priests could no longer participate in criminal trials conducted by what we would now call the secular or civil authorities.

That last instruction presents as a counterproductive instruction in the political context of the early 13th century, since it suggests the Pope was relinquishing his control over some of the laws of the land. But it is more likely that this change was intended to discredit ordeal trials in favour of the inquisitorial trial method he had sanctioned in Europe in 1206 and 1207.[6] This change was also likely intended to reinforce the Church's theological view of appropriate punishment for crime. Thus, the Pope's instruction that clerics could not pronounce or execute a sentence of death, act as judges in extreme criminal cases or administer judicial tests or ordeals,[7] was likely calculated to impose the church's anti-death-pen-

---

5   BBC, "King John and Magna Carta", *n.d.* <https://www.bbc.co.uk/bitesize/guides/zqgqtfr/revision/2>.

6   Finnbar McAuley, 'Canon Law and the End of the Ordeal', *Oxford Journal of Legal Studies*, Vol. 26, No. 3, (2006) 473, 496.

7   See Paul Halsall, Fordham University, "Medieval Sourcebook: Twelfth Ecu-

alty morality[8] on all the kings of the Holy Roman Empire in the 13th century.

While we know that the Fourth Lateran Council's prohibition on clerical involvement in criminal trials led to the expanded function of the old Norman juries, the details are not well understood. Nor do we understand exactly how English judges eventually secured control of jury deliberations four hundred years later in the 17th century – control which precipitated the development of the modern law of evidence.[9] By exploring the history of the English jury, this essay suggests that while the jury has provided democratic input into criminal law, that result is a happy coincidence and does not and should not make jury verdicts unappealable. This essay is divided into four parts.

In the first I briefly explain the political context of the twelfth and thirteenth centuries, the nature of the investiture contests, the power of Pope Innocent III over King John and other European kings and his

---

menical Council: Lateran IV 1215, Canon 18 of the Fourth Lateran Council, March 1996. <https://sourcebooks.fordham.edu/basis/lateran4.asp>. Though Pope Francis has recently changed the Catholic Catechism to ensure that Catholics understand that the death penalty is always forbidden ("New revision of number 2267 of the Catechism of the Catholic Church on the death penalty – Resciptum 'ex Audentia SS.mi'", *Summary of Bulletin*, Holy See Press Office, 2 August 2018 < http://press.vatican.va/content/salastampa/en/bollettino/pubblico/2018/08/02/180802a.html>), the church has always had an aversion to judicial punishment involving the shedding of blood. For example, in their discussion of the use of the claim of benefit of clergy which enabled transfer of clerical trials to the ecclesiastical courts for centuries, Pollock and Maitland have written, that while many punishments remained available to bishops, "the chief limit to [the bishop's] power was the elementary rule that the church would never pronounce a judgment of blood" (*The History of English Law*, 2nd ed., Cambridge University Press, 1968, Volume 1, 441). And while the Catholic Encyclopedia says that "[t]he infliction of capital punishment is not contrary to the teaching of the Catholic Church", it affirms that "[c]anon law has always forbidden clerics to shed human blood and therefore capital punishment has always been the work of the officials of the State and not of the Church" (J. Willis, "Capital Punishment" in The Catholic Encyclopedia (New York: Robert Appleton Company, 1911) <https://www.newadvent.org/cathen/12565a.htm>).

8   Ibid.

9   James B. Thayer ("The Jury and Its Development III", *Harvard Law Review*, Vol. 5, No. 8, 357, 387-388) and John H. Langbein ("The Origins of Public Prosecution at Common Law", *The American Journal of Legal History*, Vol. 17, No. 4, 313, 317) both hold that the law of evidence began its life as the law of jury control.

efforts to moralise the whole of the Holy Roman Empire. In Part Two, I summarise the Norman introduction of the Frankish jury into England for administrative purposes and why it grew and endured in criminal space. That discussion will include identification of the likely origin of the criminal jury's first function as identifier of criminals at the king's traveling assizes, but also how the jury had already begun exercising some adjudicative functions before the 13th century opened so that further jury functionality after 1215 was not such a big step as it has seemed.

In Part Three I jump four hundred years into the future and identify Queen Mary's innovation in ensuring the prosecution of criminals even when they were no longer identified by presenting juries. That innovation was necessary if those alleged to have murdered her unpopular officers were to be criminally punished since presenting juries were not always willing to perform that traditional function during her reign. I then identify why the presentation of Crown evidence in open court worked to curtail jury independence and I explain why judges were thereafter able to control jury behaviour and call out perverse verdicts. In Part Four, I connect some more dots to suggest that it is a long time since juries pushed back against unpopular executive power and functioned as democratic bulwarks of liberty. I also suggest that because juries no longer protect citizen liberty and function only as factual decision makers in criminal trial, it is doubtful that their verdicts should be any less appealable than those of trial judges.

I conclude that the criminal jury's reputation as a bulwark of liberty resulted from their push back against unpopular executive power. Since the 16th century, in criminal cases juries have functioned only as fact finders, and judges and politicians since then have curbed the evidence they hear to manage their reputation for emotional responses to prejudicial evidence. Though legislatures in Australia have begun to trust juries with more evidence since the introduction of the *Uniform Evidence Act* in 1995, since society still appears to accept that guilt in criminal cases should be proven beyond reasonable doubt, it remains reasonable that jury verdicts should be overturned if the evidence they hear does not prove guilt to that degree of certainty.

Part One - Church and State in Europe and England in the 12th and 13th centuries

It is well known that William the Conqueror adapted the jury institution to his own administrative purposes in compiling the Domesday Book in England during the 11th century. While there is still uncertainty whether the jury he so adapted was a Scandinavian or a Frankish institution or more likely an existing modification of both,[10] it is clear that the Norman jury was further adapted after it was introduced into England, to enable the identification of those suspected of crime during the 11th and 12th centuries. The first criminals the Norman kings wished to identify, were those who had assassinated occupying soldiers and officials and at the time juries were probably not local clan heads doing their civic duty, but rather representative hostages held on behalf of the collective until the perpetrators of serious crimes against the administration were identified.[11] But in time, local juries were called to provide lists of persons suspected of notorious crime against the king's peace when his judges came to town to conduct their circuit assizes.[12] The development

---

10   See for example, James B. Thayer, 'The Jury and Its Development I', *Harvard Law Review*, Vol. 5, No. 6, (1892), 249 who traces the origins of the English jury to the inquisition processes of the Carolingian kings in Germanic law (which he incorrectly refers to as the Carlovingian period), William Forsyth (*History of Trial by Jury*, John W. Parker and Son, London, 1852, 68, 193-194) who traces the jury into Anglo-Saxon practices and Ralph V. Turner ("The Origins of the Medieval English Jury: Frankish, English or Scandinavian?", *Journal of British Studies*, Vol. 7, No. 2 (1969) 1, 3-4) noting the Scandinavian origin proposals of Maitland and Vinogradoff and Hurnard's dismissal of those ideas.

11   Naomi D. Hurnard discussed the nature of Norman fines on English hundreds at length in her article "The Jury of Presentment and the Assize of Clarendon", *The English Historical Review*, Vol. 56, Issue 223, (1941), 374, 385-391. A presentment jury was a jury summoned by the king or his officers to report those who were suspected of the commission of crime, and later to advise whether those suspected of crime should be subjected to ordeal trial.

12   Hurnard (ibid) also discusses the variant opinions as to where the idea behind the English jury likely originated and settles on Frankish rather than the Scandinavian origins advocated by Paul Vinogradoff (*English Society in the Eleventh Century* (Clark, New Jersey: The LawBook Exchange Ltd, 2005, originally published by

of pre-existing forms of the jury is thus part of the idea of the rule of law and how it continued to develop in England.

Pope Innocent III's direction at the Fourth Lateran Council in 1215 that ordained priests should no longer participate in non-ecclesiastical trials anywhere in the empire – especially where capital crimes were charged – is also recognised as the primary cause of the further adaptation of the Norman jury to its fact finding role in English criminal trials in the early 13th century. But there are other, less well known developments that should be pondered before the more famous assignment of juries to fact-finding tasks can be understood. The first is the simple ecclesiastical rule that neither the Church nor its officers should be guilty of blood, meaning that the Church was opposed to the death penalty from medieval times. The second is that the Pope achieved brief but complete ascendancy over European secular rulers, including the infamous King John of England, at the very time when the Fourth Lateran Council was convened in Rome. That ascendancy is manifest in the fact that John could not insist on who should be appointed Archbishop of Canterbury as William the Conqueror had done 150 years earlier. While even the Conqueror's appointment of Lanfranc had involved risky international politics, it flowed from papal approval of his invasion of England and there was no question of a personal excommunication or an interdict invalidating all priestly service in his kingdom which Pope Innocent III later used to effectively sanction King John.

However, Pope Innocent III's use of church discipline against the English King at the beginning of the 13th century understates the crescendo which papal power had gone through in Europe during the 150 years which passed between the reigns of William and John. For not only had successive Popes succeeded in compelling kings to accept their choices

the Clarendon Press of Oxford in 1908). She also opines that Henry II's presentment jury discussed below and which was established in 1166, had connections with the communal prosecutions authorised under Ethelred's law in Saxon England. William Forsyth came to similar conclusions (infra n 19). Ethelred ruled from 978-1013 and then again from 1014 till his death in 1016.

of religious leaders in their kingdoms; the Popes had also succeeded in compelling those rulers to engage most of the able bodied of the Holy Roman Empire in the imperial war against Islam that is known to world history as the Crusades. Anyone who did not subscribe to Christianity was fair game. Anti-Semitism reached a climax during those Crusade centuries, second only to the climax Hitler achieved in the Third Reich during the Second World War. That un-Christ-like drive for dominion would likely have continued through the whole of the known world but for the defensive military prowess of the Islamic commanders in the Holy Land, Saladin most prominent among them.

King John of England was in no position to oppose Pope Innocent III. Though John might call the Pope's bluff and correctly guess that he would not physically enforce his commands, in this case sanctions worked just as well. John was bankrupt and unpopular because he had taxed the English barons to finance his doomed efforts to retain what remained of his French kingdom, and they were at the point of rebellion. John knew that the barons would not support him if the Pope did order Philip of France to continue with his invasion. And even though the Pope did order *Magna Carta* annulled because it was issued under duress just four months after it was signed at Runnymede, everyone recognised that it did accurately capture the English law of John's grandfather, and so it stuck when it was reissued without physical duress by William Marshall as regent for John's nine year old son just two years later.

The decrees of the Fourth Lateran Council however, were not directed at King John in the backwater that was England in the early 13th century. Those decrees expressed much grander designs in keeping with the spirit of Pope Innocent III's vision of a righteous world empire. If the Crusades had not been altogether successful to date, the hiatus was nothing more than a temporary pause. The laws of God's kingdom must be purified. The laws of the kingdoms which comprised God's empire on earth must conform to the doctrine of the church. Criminal law and practice must conform to the dictates of holy writ. Priests and others set apart for sacred religious service must not have blood on their hands and the Pope placed a premium upon clerical integrity.[13] Though priests in many nations were already observing earlier papal bans on the use of confessional information other than for penitential purposes, the seal of confession was made binding for the first time on the entire church.[14] But the Pope did not outlaw ordeal trial directly. He simply banned priestly involvement in ordeal trials. Finnbar McAuley has explained the subtlety of the international politics involved. Rather than ban the ordeal outright

> the Pope took the prudent course of confining his ruling against it to a ban on priestly involvement in its administration, thereby avoiding unnecessary damage to the spirit of *détente* which had been developing between the civil and ecclesiastical authorities in the decades following the shocking murder of archbishop [sic] Becket in 1170...the new dispensation turned on the establishment of an auxiliary procedure designed to remove the need to remit hard cases *ad iudicorum Dei*...the idea [being] that trial *per inquisitionem* would render the ordeal surplus to requirements.[15]

McAuley is also certain in that spirit of détente, that Pope Innocent III was not making an unashamed grab for sole jurisdiction over all criminal matters in what remained of the Holy Roman Empire when he banned clerical involvement in the ordeal in 1215. Rather he was correcting a vulgar, superstitious and unscriptural practice which had involved the clergy in all manner of corruption.[16]

While Pope Innocent III intended to regain spiritual control of the clergy, his ban on clerical involvement did not proceed with reckless disregard for criminal process outside ecclesiastical courts. The new *forma juramenti* oaths which he had authorised in decretals issued in 1206 and

---

13   Finnbar McAuley confirms the Fourth Lateran Council reforms were part of Pope Innocent III's drive for clerical integrity, but explains that the blood the Council sought to remove from clerical hands was probably not the blood shed in legal capital cases, but rather that shed in soldiery (surgery) (McAuley (n 6), 473, 484, 491, 498 and 507).

14   A. Keith Thompson, *Religious Confession and the Common Law* (Martinus Nihjoff, Leiden, 2011), Chapter Three.

15   McAuley (n 6), 499-500.

16   Ibid (n 6), 477-483, 493.

1207, enabled secular judges in the Italian city states and other European polities, "to probe the veracity of the accused's protestations of innocence."[17] But in England, where King Henry II had developed the ancient jury idea in the *Constitutions and Assize of Clarendon* in 1166 and the *Assize of Northampton* in 1176,[18] it was not necessary to move to the inquisitorial process the Pope had effectively recommended in Europe in 1206 and 1207. The English adaptation of the jury to new criminal functions in the wake of the effective papal ban on ordeal trials in 1215 are the subject of Part Two.

Part Two - Adaptation of the Norman jury to criminal presentation and fact-finding in the 12th and 13th centuries

Criminal processes were different in England than in the rest of Europe, particularly after the Norman conquest. In England, the population had become accustomed to the idea that their peers should be involved in trial process. In Europe, trial process and interrogation was mostly left to the king's officials. Thus, Pope Innocent III's decretals authorising inquisitorial methods to deal with all cases of crime, did not provide an obvious and attractive alternative criminal process in England when ordeal trials were practically outlawed.

The idea that senior locals were a reliable source of criminal intelligence, was not a Norman insight. William Forsyth says that accusations had been made in criminal trials under the laws of Ethelred (reigned 978-1013 and 1014-1016), and twelve senior thanes were required to act as public prosecutors with "the duty of discovering and presenting the perpetrators of all crimes within their district."[19] But Forsyth had earlier

---

17   Ibid 496.
18   Hurnard (n 11). She explains that the English presentment jury had been borrowed from Francia and had antecedents in the practice of Ethelred in the 10th century, but had been adapted by the Normans who added community fines to ensure the apprehension of those who murdered occupying soldiers (377-390).
19   William Forsyth, *History of Trial by Jury,* (John W. Parker and Son, West Strand,

doubted whether this duty in Ethelred's law counted as proof that the origins of the jury might be found in Anglo-Saxon practice.[20] However, if Ethelred's law does prove that the English jury had Anglo-Saxon as well as Norman antecedents, then the Norman innovation was to use the Anglo-Saxon presentment jury for administrative purposes.[21] While the Anglo-Saxon jury institution appears to have been popular because it captured community sentiment, it was still subject to abuse since it was susceptible to rumour and vendetta which could found criminal prosecutions. The Norman introduction of trial by battle in criminal cases also appears to have discouraged the neighbourhood communication which was the foundation of the Anglo-Saxon presentment jury since accusers were not keen to fight with notorious criminals.[22]

The consequence was that Henry II (reigned 1154-1189) began the reformation of criminal law in the *Assize* and *Constitutions of Clarendon* in 1164 and 1166 and again in the *Assize of Northampton* in 1176. While it is difficult to separate out the nature of each of his innovations in those three separate legislative acts, Peter Leeson's insight helps. He says that the adap-

---

London, 1852), 193-194.

20   Ibid 67-68 where he noted that Sir Francis Palgrave thought the connection was obvious. Naomi Hurnard noted further that while the "Saxon, Danish, and Norman kings all took measures to secure the arrest and punishment of criminals" and that Ethelred's system of presentment remained unchanged through into Norman times, the Saxon kings probably "borrowed this practice of communal accusation from Francia" "[w]ithout adopting the whole system of inquest and recognition" (Hurnard (n 11), 374, 376-378. Forsyth manifests his own uncertainty about the Anglo-Saxon origin of the jury as it developed from Norman times when he says

> This office, however, seems to have fallen into abeyance, at all events after the invasion of the Normans; and accusations of crime were left to the general voice of the neighbourhood denouncing the guilt of the suspected person (ibid, 194).

21   Thayer, *The Jury 1* (n 10), 249, 251-252. See also Clarance Ray Jeffery, "The Development of Crime in Early English Society", *The Journal of Criminal Law, Criminology, and Police Science,* Vol. 47, Issue 6 (1957) 647, 653, 659.

22   The Normans introduced trial by battle almost immediately after the conquest. Trial by battle in land matters only lasted till 1179 when King Henry II abolished it in the Council of Windsor (Peter T. Leeson, 'Trial by Battle', *Journal of Legal Analysis,* Vol.3, No. 1 (2011), 341, 369). Leeson refers readers to Russell, Selden, Gibson and Neilson for information about trial by battle in criminal matters in his third footnote. Trial by battle endured as an alternative way of settling some criminal disputes until at least the 15th century. See also Thayer, *The Jury I* (n 10), 263-264, 267 and Jeffery (n 21), 659 and 661.

tation of William the Conqueror's inquisitorial jury (which was used after 1066 to work out property values so the king could decide how much tax he could levy) to determine land disputes following the Council of Windsor in 1179, practically ended trial by battle. That insight confirms the popularity and utility of the inquisitorial jury as a late twelfth century dispute resolution mechanism fifty years before Pope Innocent III removed the ordeal from all European criminal jurisdictions.[23]

Naomi Hurnard carefully analysed Henry II's jury reforms between 1164 and 1176 in 1941 and no one has seriously doubted her analysis or conclusions since.[24] She began by assessing the existing scholarship as to whether the jury had Anglo-Saxon, Scandinavian or Frankish origins and concluded that the presentment jury at least, had been used in criminal matters during the reign of Ethelred at the end of the 10th century. But as Thayer had explained at the end of the 19th century, the Normans had used it for administrative purposes in a manner reminiscent of the European *inquisitio* when they compiled the Domesday Book in the 11th century.[25] Thayer said Henry II organized the previous irregular use of

---

23   Leeson (n 22), 369. Leeson explained:
      That council introduced the grand assize as an alternative to trial by battle in
      real property cases. The new law gave tenants an option: a tenant who didn't
      want judicial combat to decide his land dispute could put himself on the
      judgment of his countrymen instead. The grand assize consisted of twelve
      knights of the shire. It replaced trial by battle with trial by jury.
      The overall tenor of Leeson's argument was that trial by battle was an econom-
      ically efficient way of disposing of disputes about land ownership until a more
      efficient new method was developed. Trial by battle was efficient before trial by
      jury because it allocated "contested property to the higher bidder in an all-pay
      auction" (ibid 341). It also provided an acceptable spectacle to neighbours when
      true ownership was unclear (ibid 342).
24   Note in particular Ralph V. Turner's deference to her scholarship summarising
      jury origins in 1968. Turner preferred her reasoning over various other legal his-
      torians including Haskins and Maitland and said her analysis was "convincing"
      (Turner (n 10) 1, 3-5, 7-10. Helmholz discusses the prevalence of Hurnard's view
      and Van Caenegem's criticisms but ultimately concludes that the disagreement is
      only about emphasis and whether Henry II's law and order measures from 1166
      should be seen as innovative or mere continuations of existing Anglo-Saxon
      institutions (R. H. Helmholz, "The Early History of the Grand Jury and Canon
      Law", *The University of Chicago Law Review*, Vol. 50, No. 2, Fiftieth Anniversary
      Issue (Spring 1983), 613, 614-616, 626).
25   Thayer, *The Jury I* (n 10), 249, 251-252.

the jury as an inquisition tool in "the text of certain of his ordinances (assizes)"[26] and shows how a jury was used to determine whether the towns of Wallingford/Oxford or Abingdon had the prior right to hold a market.[27] However, Hurnard explained Henry II's legislative innovations in much more detail.

Hurnard explained that the Normans had introduced a system of fining the hundred if a Norman was killed and the institutionalised Anglo-Saxon presentment jury had not accused anyone of the crime.[28] There was no fine in the case of the murder of a proven Englishman. But there were also practices that allowed persons of well-known bad character to be sent directly to ordeal trial when they were accused of serious crime. Persons of better character could avoid the ordeal by compurgation (essentially calling character witness), unless there were three or more accusers in accordance with the old biblical rules.[29] But Henry II changed all those rules in his assizes and insisted that jury accusations should result in ordeal trials in every case, unless there was no question of guilt. In those certain cases he provided that punishment should follow without further ado.[30] There was also a requirement that those accused by the presentment jury, but who succeeded at the ordeal, must abjure the realm.[31] These were the innovations of a king pursuing a law and order agenda with a vengeance. In the words of Naomi Hurnard,

> at every point the assize [of Clarendon 1166] tightens up the procedure for dealing with robbers, murderers, and thieves; where before no more severe proof than compurgation has been required, now there will be ordeal; and even success at the ordeal is not to bring complete impunity; where there has been ordeal the testi-

---

26   Ibid 254.
27   Ibid 254-255.
28   Hurnard (n 11), 385, 390.
29   Ibid 393-394. Note that the Mosaic Law in the Old Testament of the Bible (Deuteronomy 17:5, 6 and 19:15) was reiterated in the Christian New Testament (for example, Matthew 18:16, 2 Corinthians 13:1, I Timothy 5:19 and Hebrews 10:28).
30   Hurnard (n 11), 396.
31   Ibid 397.

mony of jurors is now to be accepted as final.[32]

Hurnard also thought that the *Assize of Clarendon* denied manorial lords the right to replicate these remedies and thus to assure all the profits to the king as the proceeds of his judicial process.[33] And as is more well known, in these several law reforms named for Clarendon, Henry II also sought to deny exemption on grounds of clerical status to those accused of crime.[34] This was the well-known beginning of his argument with Archbishop Thomas Becket who opposed this assertion of jurisdiction over clerics by the King on double jeopardy grounds.[35] Ten years later, perhaps because of the success of his tougher stance on serious crime, King Henry II made further retrospective rule changes (the *Assize of Northampton*) which applied the Clarendon rules to lesser crimes - lesser criminals might now stay in England if they successfully negotiated their way through an ordeal trial, but without a foot or some other member of the body as punishment.[36]

The bottom line for King Henry II thus seems to have been that if it was good enough for a jury of twelve good men to accuse anyone of crime, it was good enough for him. The seemingly automatic referral of those accused by presenting juries to ordeal after 1166, also provides English context for the changes that followed the effective abolition of ordeal by Pope Innocent III at the Fourth Lateran Council in 1215. Though the Pope had established an alternative proof procedure in criminal matters in Europe between 1206 and 1207,[37] King Henry II in England had given the presenting jury his imprimatur as a fact finding institution from 1166, and he had successfully increased its jurisdiction in 1176.[38] Hurnard has

---

32   Ibid.

33   Ibid 398.

34   Ibid 399.

35   Harold Berman, *Law and Revolution: The Formation of the Western Legal Tradition* (Harvard University Press, 1983) 185-186.

36   Hurnard (n 11), 396.

37   McAuley (n 6).

38   Note however that Richard Helmholz is certain that King Henry II's effort to take control of all criminal jurisdiction through his Assizes of Clarendon and Northampton in 1166 and 1176 were not immediately successful. The ecclesiasti-

summarised that although Henry II's reforms seem to have been targeted at "professional thievery and brigandage"[39] and proceeded on simple suspicion,[40] they succeeded because they were "based on the traditional system of communal accusation."[41]

However, there was another element to Henry II's development of the jury before his death at the end of the 12th century that needs to be noticed before we move on. American historians see in this early development, the differentiation they retain to this day between the grand jury and the petty jury. In this medieval time period, there were two different juries - the jury that accused people of crime, and the jury that decided whether they were guilty or not. No one is completely clear on how and when this differentiation happened. That is, no one knows at what point the jury began to be asked not just who was suspected of crime in their hundred, but whether they were guilty or not. The Encyclopedia Brittanica attributes this change to the *English Articles of Visitation* in 1194 but does not provide references or explain what those Articles said and how that direction changed the function of the jury.[42] Thomas A. Green, mostly relying on the outdated opinions of Maitland, but also summarising recent research by Groot about the historical origins of the jury, says:

> Our best guess is that the hundredmen made presentments…and then exercised discretionary power in the subsequent task of stating who they truly suspected…In private law the grand and petty juries came to dominate; on the criminal side, the jury of presentment was in frequent use. All of these juries, save for the presenting jury, rendered verdicts on the subject of guilt or innocence,

---

cal courts retained criminal jurisdiction in many matters of crime for a variety of reasons including that the royal courts provided an inadequate forum or remedy, and when some form of private settlement remained desirable (R.H. Helmholz, "Compurgation and the Courts of the Medieval Church", *Law and History Review*, Vol. 1, No. 1 (1983) 1, 11, 23-24.

39   Hurnard (n 11), 405.

40   Ibid 408.

41   Ibid 410.

42   The Editors of Encyclopedia Britannica, "Petit jury", *n.d.* < https://www.britannica.com/topic/petit-jury#ref181484>.

or on some other dispositive question of fact...By 1215...there was ample precedent for putting substantial laymen on oath to say whether or not a suspect was guilty of felony.[43]

Groot's research into late 12th century cases is detailed. He suggested "that the ease with which the English went into the jury system was attributable to the prior development of the jury in private as well as public prosecutions."[44] Groot observes that in the period between the *Assize of Clarendon* in 1166 and the abolition of the ordeal in 1215, juries had already been discriminating between those persons accused of crime who should go straight to the ordeal and those who might be acquitted if they could find sufficient compurgators to confirm that their oaths of innocence were trustworthy.[45] Not only were jurors opining about the mental state of the persons they had accused of crime in 1199 and 1212 Stafford and Yorkshire cases, they were generally opining about the accuracy of accusations they had brought before justices in eyre and deciding what form of proof should be required after consulting with jurors from the vill where the events had occurred.[46] This accepted practice, plus the fact that juries that made mistakes or changed their minds about an accusation, were neither fined nor punished, "granted [those jurors] a significant power to adjudicate – to say that a defendant, although the subject of suspicion, was not guilty."[47] Thus before 1215, English juries were already exercising discretion which came very close to judgment and re-

---

43   Thomas A. Green, "The Transformation of Jury Trial in Early Modern England" in *Verdict according to conscience: perspective on the English criminal jury trial 1200-1800* (University of Chicago Press, 1985), 10-13. The hundred was a unit of government and taxation in English medieval government between the village (vill) and the shire or county, and originally appears to have included one hundred peasant families. The hundredmen were those responsible for the administration of law and order within the hundreds (see for example "Anglo-Saxon and Norman society pre-1066", *n.d.*, BBC <https://www.bbc.co.uk/bitesize/guides/zq38tyc/revision/1>).

44   Roger A. Groot, "The Jury in Private Criminal Prosecutions before 1215", *The American Journal of Legal History*, Vol. 27, No. 2 (1983) 113. Justices in eyre were the justices dispatched by the King on circuits to provide royal justice throughout his kingdom. A vill was the smallest unit in medieval English administration and is roughly equivalent to the idea of village or parish.

45   Roger A. Groot, "The Jury of Presentment before 1215, *The American Journal of Legal History*, Vol. 26, No. 1 (1983), 1, 10.

46   Ibid 11-14.

47   Ibid 21-22.

flected the "[s]ignificant distrust of the ordeal as a mode of proof" since the reign of William Rufus (reigned 1087-1100).[48] For Groot and Green, this innovative use of the jury "harnessed the prestige and knowledge of the most respected members of local communities"[49] and avoided the inquisition in place of the ordeal which came to rely on tortured confessions as the primary proof of guilt in criminal cases in Europe after 1215.[50]

While Maitland and others have suggested that the adjudicative functions which English juries began to exercise between the *Assize of Clarendon* in 1166 and the Fourth Lateran Council in 1215 was actually the work of a second jury,[51] no eminent historian doubts that it smoothed the transition to jury verdicts which followed. Indeed, Green has even suggested that "the divine aspect of the ordeal...[may] have attached to the [jury and its decisions] when it replaced the ordeal after 1215."[52] Whether jury verdicts were ever regarded as the declaration of the will of God is a question beyond the scope of this essay. However, it was a small step for the king's justices to ask juries to adjudicate guilt or innocence instead of having a priest administer an ordeal when they were instructed "to make such experiments as they saw fit and gradually feel their way towards a solution."[53] And, in due course, official recognition of jury decisions in criminal cases, made their decisions close to invincible for several hundred years, but that is a different story. In Part Three I explain how juries lost their invincibility.

48   Ibid 22.
49   Green (n 43), 10.
50   Groot (n 44), 1 relying on John H. Langbein, *Torture and the Law of Proof, England and Europe in the Ancien Regime* (University of Chicago Press, 1976), 5-8.
51   F. W. Maitland, *The Constitutional History of England* (Cambridge at the University Press, 1919) 128.
52   Green (n 43), 19. See also Larry T. Bates "Trial by Jury after Williams v Florida", *Hamline Law Review* Vol. 10, No. 1 (1987) 53, 62 and Hurnard (n 11), 408.
53   T.F.T. Plucknett, *A Concise History of the Common Law*, (Little Brown and Co., 5th edition 1956, Boston) 119.

Part Three – Queen Mary's innovation with prosecutors and public review of criminal facts

Langbein suggests that it is still unclear how medieval juries became "passive courtroom triers",[54] but in the light of Langbein's insights, Green is confident that transformation hinged on the rise of public prosecutors in the late sixteenth century.[55] Though previous statutory and judicial attempts to control self-informing juries had utterly failed, the appointment of officials to back up presenting juries in the accusation of suspected criminals,[56] necessitated the public communication of criminal facts in court which jurors did not know beforehand. And it is no coincidence that these reforms took place by statute during the reign of Henry VIII's oldest daughter Mary. As is well known, she moved rapidly to reinstate the Roman Catholic Church as the established Church of the State, and she presided over the execution of Thomas Cranmer, the Archbishop of Canterbury for heresy on 21 March 1556.[57] She was hugely unpopular and though many of her officials were murdered, the accusations of assassins by or to presenting juries dried up during her reign. She had to defend her administration and the officials she had appointed to run her government, and so she passed the Marian bail[58] and committal statutes.[59] Presenting juries could still initiate criminal prosecutions, but if they did not, these statutes ensured there were still prosecutions because these statutes imposed obligations on Justices of the Peace to investigate and imprison suspects if there was a chance they would turn fugitive.[60]

---

54   John H. Langbein, "The Origins of Public Prosecution at Common Law", *The American Journal of Legal History*, Vol. 17, No. 4 (1973), 313, 314.

55   Thomas A. Green, *Verdict according to Conscience: Perspectives on the English Criminal Jury Trial 1200-1800* (University of Chicago Press, 1985), 105-106.

56   Ibid 182.

57   Diarmaid MacCulloch, *Thomas Cranmer, A Life* (Yale University Press, 1998), 604.

58   1 & 2 Phil & Mary c. 13 (1554-1554).

59   2 & 3 Phil & Mary c. 10 (1555).

60   Langbein (n 54), 320. It is interesting to ponder whether she and her advisors considered reinstating the fines on hundreds by which the Norman conquerors had forced presenting juries to identify those who murdered Norman officials during the 11th and 12th centuries. As it turned out, the establishment of official government prosecutors yielded unexpected collateral benefits in enabling judicial control

Langbein says the statutes were a response to growing jury passivity.[61] The new bail procedure required two Justices of the Peace to examine the prisoner and those that had brought him to their attention, decide whether he was a flight risk or not and record their findings in writing for the assize judges when they came to town to run formal trials. There was no need to bind over those who were not granted bail.[62] While Justices of the Peace had been deciding bail cases already, the new process required two to officiate in all cases in the future and the record required, subjected them to the oversight of the King's Justices. The new committal statute further required the Justices of the Peace officiating at bail hearings, to bind informants and potential witnesses to attend the expected trials with bonds that could be forfeited if they did not appear. As Langbein puts it,

> The examining JP was being formally instructed to gather evidence for trial and to bind witnesses. The Marian committal statute was employing the procedure of the bail statute to a radically different end. The bail statute intended to deter or to detect and punish a corrupt practice among a relative handful of JPs. The committal statute turned the pretrial investigation into a device for the prosecution at trial in every case of felony in the realm.[63]

Justices of the peace were chosen as Queen Mary's prosecutors because "well before the Marian statutes the justices of the peace were the officers to whom aggrieved citizens would make complaint of serious crime."[64] But though the Justices of the Peace were only made back-up prosecutors to presenting juries, the new statutes enabled Mary's officials to force her Justices of the Peace to "investigate, bind witnesses, and appear at assizes to orchestrate prosecution."[65] At those trials, Justices of the Peace would not only testify about their investigations. They

---

of juries that had been close to a law unto themselves since they were officially confirmed as finders of fact during the reign of Henry III in the 13th century.

61   Ibid 317.
62   Green (n 43), 110.
63   Langbein (n 54), 321.
64   Ibid 319.
65   Ibid.

would also cross-examine the accused before the jury.[66] The obligation pressed upon Justices of the Peace to perform these duties was effective because the early Tudors "employed the Council and the court [sic] of Star Chamber to monitor the actions of royal officials" and to discipline abuse.[67] Green has confirmed that individual jurors and even whole juries could be disciplined in the same manner.

The development of the role of public prosecutor reduced jury discretion.[68] While the jury became passive in part because it could not be informed about all the crime perpetrated by roving gangs of professional thieves,[69] as Crown officials took "responsibility for initiation and prosecution of criminal cases and for the management of the trial itself",[70] juries retreated to their role as deciders of the facts of the cases they heard.[71] Because more and more evidence was heard in open court, juries lacked the power to "manipulate the evidence"[72] and they could be disciplined if they tried to do so, on judicial referral.

The establishment of an official prosecution thus changed the balance of power between the jury and the judge. Because much more evidence was heard in open court, "[t]he judge was armed with evidence that he could use to challenge the accused" and the jury.[73] Because the jury lost control of the evidence, it could no longer conceal or alter it.[74] Similarly, because all the facts were discussed in the presence of the judge in open court, the judge was in a better position to oversee the verdict and how or if it was consistent with the evidence.[75] In a very real sense, the Marian bail

---

66   Ibid.
67   Green (n 43), 113.
68   Robert C. Palmer, "Review: Conscience and the Law: The English Criminal Jury Reviewed Work(s): Verdict According to Conscience by Thomas Andrew Green" (1986) 84 *Michigan Law Review* 787, 789.
69   Green (n 43), 126.
70   Ibid 106.
71   Ibid 108-109.
72   Ibid 106.
73   Ibid 110.
74   Palmer (n 68), 789.
75   Thomas A. Green, 'The Jury and the English Law of Homicide', 1200-1600',

and committal statutes thus heralded the advent of the modern law of evidence, which as Langbein says is the law of jury control.[76]

Thomas Green says that English juries were regarded as a bulwark of liberty because they "prevented the imposition of sanctions they deemed too harsh".[77] While there is evidence that English juries continued to moderate executive power and that perverse verdicts continued to ex-ert criminal law reform pressure long after these Marian criminal law innovations, it is doubtful that the institutional jury has been as signif-icant an influence in the democratisation of criminal justice since those changes in the 16th century. In Part Four I relate these historical insights to the almost sacred respect which continues to be accorded to the jury as an institution, and question whether jury verdicts should be any less appealable than other judicial decisions.

The point of this discussion is to discredit the idea that everything about the jury is sacrosanct, and to affirm instead, that we can adjust the func-tions and operation of criminal juries without irreparably damaging the delivery of justice in modern society. Indeed, this historical treatment is intended to convince that we should experiment more with criminal jury practice in Australia – to seed ideas, including whether unanimity is necessary, whether juries should have to give more than yes or no an-swers, whether we would irreparably damage the delivery of criminal justice if we professionalised and paid smaller lay juries, and whether

---

(1976) 74 *Michigan Law Review* 413, 490.

76   Langbein (n 54), 317. Thayer (*The Jury III* (n 9) 387-388) has written:

> [T]he greatest and most characteristic offshoot of the jury was that body of excluding rules which chiefly constitutes the English "Law of Evidence". If we imagine what would have happened if the petit jury had kept up the older methods of procedure, as the grand jury in criminal cases did, and does at the present day [in the United States], - if, instead of hearing witness publicly, under the eye of the judge, it had heard them privately and without any judicial supervision, it is easy to see that our law of evidence would never have grown up. This it is, - this judicial oversight and control of the process of introducing evidence to the jury, that gave it birth; and he who would understand it must keep this fact constantly in mind.

77   Green (n 43), 105.

their decision making should be reviewable on grounds other than the possibility that an innocent person had been wrongly convicted.

But note I am not suggesting that we completely do away with the jury or that because judges and other public officials are more efficient, they better deliver popular justice. The primary reason that the jury has endured as an Anglo-American trial institution despite official inquisitorial alternatives, seems to lie in its democratisation of the criminal process. Though we may need additional measures to prevent jury objectivity being corrupted by media opinion, we do not want to completely do away with lay criminal justice because officials deciding criminal cases are just as susceptible to media opinion, and they can become cynical when processing cases day in and day out.

Part Four – Should jury decisions be sacred in the 21st century?

This brief discussion of the origins of the English jury and the beginning of the loss of its independence, confirm that its reputation as a democratic bulwark of liberty[78] was a fortuitous accident. It also suggests that the jury was realistically, the most convenient politically correct way to deliver criminal justice when the king was asserting his supremacy, but at a time when the people were suspicious about his motives.[79] Several leading historians believe that medieval English people were already sceptical of the ordeal as a method of proof[80] when Pope Innocent III outlawed it in 1215. They suggest that medieval English people were more alert to irrationality in their criminal processes than 21st century people living in common law jurisdictions expect.

---

78   See for example, Lord Devlin, *Trial by Jury* (Methuen, 1956) 164.
79   See Green above at notes 49 and 77 and supporting text.
80   See for example McAuley (n 6), 473, 477, 508-511. McAuley notes the similar views of R. Bartlett, *Trial by Fire and Water, The Medieval Judicial Ordeal* (Clarendon Press, 1986) 86 though he notes at his footnote 232 that Colman, Hyams, Arnold et al., Kieckhofer, Radding and Brown were prepared to countenance other views.

While for the most part the advent of the jury as an English criminal trial institution has been a happy accident that has moderated the harshness of punishment in English criminal law and even forced legislative amendment,[81] it is doubtful that its decisions deserve the sacrosanctity that history accords them. For just as medieval presentment juries could be corrupted by rumour, intimidation and bribery,[82] and Tudor and later petit juries could be emotionally misled by unreliable evidence,[83] so modern juries can be swayed by untested opinion and even hysteria in modern social media.[84] If it was legitimate to amerce (fine) Tudor juries for various misconduct and perverse verdicts,[85] is our modern legislative and judicial reluctance to revisit jury verdicts justified?

In the final part of this essay, I therefore revisit the current Australian jurisprudence which sets out the grounds upon which jury verdicts can be appealed with particular reference to the High Court decision in the *Chamberlain*,[86] *M v The Queen*[87] and *Pell* cases.[88]

The facts of the *Chamberlain* and *Pell* cases are so well known that I do

---

81 Sir William Holdsworth has noted Blackstone's indiscriminate praise of all the laws and institutions of England (*A History of English Law*, 2nd ed., (Boston, Little Brown and Co., 1923) Vol 2, 302) and said of Benefit of Clergy, that it became "by gradual mutations…a merciful mitigation of the general law with respect to capital punishments" (William Blackstone, *Commentaries on the Law of England* (New York and London, Garland Publishing Co., 1978), Vol. 1, 364). See also Green (n 43) and n 77.

82 Forsyth (n 19) notes the care that was taken by Englishmen in Norman times about making accusations, particularly after the introduction of trial by battle, for few wanted to run the risk of a challenge to make good an accusation in a battle. In this context, accusations by a jury spread the risk (ibid 192-198(194))

83 Note Thayer's discussion of the methods by which corrupt jurors could be punished, particularly between the 14th and 17th centuries (*The Jury III*, n 9).

84 Note that in the original 1900 version of the *Crimes Act* (NSW), s 577 provided that a judge could order a change of venue for the trial if satisfied that the accused could not get a fair trial at the original place where the trial was to be convened. This rule anticipates juror prejudice sourced in public knowledge including from media and social media sources. This rule is perpetuated in s 30 of the *Criminal Procedure Act 1986* (NSW).

85 Thayer, *The Jury III* (n 9).

86 *Chamberlain v The Queen (No 2)* (1984) 153 CLR 521 (*Chamberlain*).

87 *M v The Queen* (1994) 181 CLR 487.

88 *Pell v The Queen* [2020] HCA 12.

not need to set them out in detail. Suffice to say, that Lindy Chamberlain was convicted of the murder of her daughter Azariah near Ayers Rock in Australia's Northern Territory in 1982, and Cardinal George Pell was convicted of the sexual abuse of two altar boys in 1996 in the Victorian County Court in 2019. M had been charged with the sexual assault of his 13 year old daughter and had been convicted solely on the basis of her inconsistent and sometimes implausible evidence. In the M and *Pell* High Court appeals, the High Court considered that the juries should have had reasonable doubts about the guilt of the accused. Lindy Chamberlain was eventually pardoned as a result of the recommendations of the Morling Royal Commission even though two separate High Court panels had affirmed her conviction. It is noteworthy that the first jury which considered Cardinal Pell's case could not reach a decision and was discharged.[89] The High Court decision in the *Chamberlain* case featured a strong dissent from Sir William Deane and the Victorian Court of Appeal decision affirming Cardinal Pell's conviction similarly featured a strong dissent by Justice Mark Weinberg.

The High Court's restatement of the law as to when and how a jury verdict could be overturned on appeal in M v *The Queen* in 1994[90] was the first time it had an opportunity to revisit that law after the Morling Royal Commission recommended that Lindy Chamberlain's conviction was unsafe in light of new evidence.[91] Those justices then said that each appellate judge

---

89 Note that there is no evidence that the second County Court jury in the *Pell* case was psychographically profiled by the Police or Prosecution, or that it was unduly influenced to convict during the trial process in any way. Thus, it is assumed that both the Prosecution and Defence were presented with the list of potential jurors at the same time on the morning of the trial. In earlier ages of English history, the Crown sometimes achieved the result it desired by packing, threatening or even bribing juries (Robert J East, "Jury Packing: A Thing of the Past?", 48(5) *The Modern Law Review* (Sept. 1985) 518).

90 The law the High Court was interpreting in M v *The Queen* was s 6(1) of the *Criminal Appeal Act 1912* (NSW).

91 The new evidence that prompted the establishment of the Morling Royal Commission into the conviction of Lindy Chamberlain, was the discovery of Azaria's matinee jacket by Police searching for a missing English tourist near the foot of Ayers Rock three years after all her appeals had been concluded (Neda Vanovac and Dijana Damjanovic, "Azaria Chamberlain: Newly released NT cabinet documents detail decision to review convictions", January 1, 2017 *ABC News* <https://www.abc.net.au/news/2017-01-01/azaria-chamberlain-and-1986-cab-

must make an independent assessment as to whether there is a reasonable doubt of the guilt of the appellant having regard to all of the evidence.[92] The point is not whether the appellate court entertains a reasonable doubt, for that would substitute the appellate court's assessment of the evidence for the jury's assessment without the benefit of having heard that evidence first hand. After making proper allowance for the jury's advantage in hearing all the evidence first hand, the appellate court is required to determine whether there remains a 'significant possibility that an innocent person has been convicted'. If that possibility existed, 'then the court is bound to act and to set aside a verdict based upon that evidence.'[93]

In *Chamberlain*, the majority had found that the jury's power to decide the facts was too important to interfere with. Gibbs CJ and Mason J said:

> The responsibility of deciding upon the verdict, whether of conviction or acquittal, lies with the jury and we can see no justification, in the absence of express statutory provisions leading to a different result, for an appellate tribunal to usurp the function of the jury and disturb a verdict of conviction simply because it disagrees with the jury's conclusion ... the trial is by jury, and (absent other sources of error) the jury's verdict should not be interfered with unless the Court of Criminal Appeal concludes that a reasonable jury ought to have had a reasonable doubt.[94]

In dissent, Justice Murphy observed that although "the jury was a strong antidote to the elitist tendencies of the legal system" and was "the means by which the people participate in the administration of justice", juries do make mistakes and convict innocent people. The conferral of power on appeal courts to set aside unsafe convictions even when those convictions were the result of jury decisions "operate[d] as a further safeguard against the mistaken conviction of the innocent."[95] In his dissent, Sir William Deane said that the continuing community acceptance of the le-

---

inet-documents-released/8152774>).

92   *M v The Queen* (n 87) 492 (Mason CJ, Deane, Dawson and Toohey JJ).
93   Ibid 494.
94   *Chamberlain* (n 86) 534.
95   Ibid 569.

gitimacy of trial by jury would be damaged if their verdicts could not be examined and overturned when necessary.[96] Any other approach would be to entrench the possibility of injustice.[97] The conviction of innocent people would undermine the credibility of the legal system as a whole.

In his dissent in the Victorian Court of Appeal in *Pell*, Weinberg J essentially followed Sir William Deane in *Chamberlain*. He would have acquitted Cardinal Pell because there was a 'significant possibility that the applicant in this case may not have committed these offences.'[98] Sir William Deane added another observation in *Kingswell v R* that is relevant in this brief consideration of the continued relevance and legitimacy of the English jury within our system of criminal justice. He said that the combination of random selection of jurors, the confidentiality of the jury's deliberative process, and the 'insistence upon its function of determining the particular charge according to the evidence', is supposed to offer assurance to the accused that he or she will not be judged by 'self-righteous pre-trial publicity or the passions of the mob.'[99]

Though we strive for better conviction statistics than Thomas Green said were delivered by the justice system in the 13th century,[100] it remains doubtful whether Australian society wants higher conviction rates if an unacceptably high number of the innocent are caught along with Lindy Chamberlain in the conviction net. As Sir William Deane has opined, that risk will inevitably bring the criminal justice system as a whole into disrepute.[101]

In its unanimous decision overturning the majority of the Victorian Court of Appeal in the *Pell* case, the High Court restated the law:

> The function of the court of criminal appeal...in a case such as the

---

96   Ibid 617.
97   Ibid 618.
98   *Pell v The Queen* [2019] VSCA 186, 307 [1111].
99   *Kingswell v R* (1985) 159 CLR 264, 302.
100   Green (n 43) 106-107.
101   *Chamberlain* (n 86) 617-618.

present, proceeds upon the assumption that the evidence of the complainant was assessed by the jury to be credible and reliable. The court examines the record to see whether, notwithstanding that assessment – either by reason of inconsistencies, discrepancies or other inadequacy; or in light of other evidence – the court is satisfied that the jury, actually rationally, ought nonetheless to have entertained a reasonable doubt as to proof of guilt.[102]

Those justices then applied that law to the facts of Cardinal Pell's appeal:

> [T]he issue for the Court of Appeal was whether the compounding improbabilities caused by the unchallenged evidence...required the jury, acting rationally, to have entertained a doubt as to the applicant's guilt...Making full allowance for the advantages enjoyed by the jury, there is a significant possibility...that an innocent party has been convicted.[103]

Since the Victorian Court of Appeal had reviewed all the recorded evidence the second jury had heard,[104] the High Court also explained the difference between the function of the Court of Appeal reviewing a jury verdict, and the task of the jury at trial:

> [T]he performance by a court of criminal appeal of its functions does not involve the substitution of trial by an appeal court for trial by a jury, so...the appeal court should not seek to duplicate the function of the jury in its assessment of the credibility of the witnesses where that assessment is dependent upon the evaluation of the witnesses in the witness-box. The jury performs its function on the basis that its decisions are made unanimously, and

---

102   *Pell* (n 88) [39].

103   Ibid [119].

104   Cardinal Pell was first tried in Magistrate Court in Victoria in 2017 without a result because even when the Magistrate told the jury it could reach a majority verdict, those jurors could not (*Pell* (n 96) [356]; *Pell* (n 88) [3]). The evidence at the first trial was recorded. During the second jury trial in 2018 also in the Magistrates Court, the second jury which convicted the Cardinal did not hear personally, the evidence of Witness A whom the majority of the Victorian Court of Appeal assessed as a "compellingly credible witness" (*Pell* (n 88) [5]). They heard only the evidence he gave at the first jury trial. When the Victorian Court of Appeal considered the appeal, they watched the evidence of Witness A as recorded at the first jury trial, along with "a number of other prosecution witnesses" (*Pell* (n 88) [5]).

after the benefit of sharing the jurors' subjective assessments of the witnesses. Judges of courts of criminal appeal do not perform the same function in the same way as the jury, or with the same advantages that the jury brings to the discharge of its function...The assessment of the weight to be accorded to a witness' evidence by reference to the manner in which it was given by the witness has always been, and remains, the province of the jury.[105]

The error made by the majority in the Victorian Court of Appeal was to decide whether the jury came to a verdict that was subjectively reasonable rather than objectively deciding whether that verdict was rational and reasonable in light of all the contradictory evidence they heard.[106] Objectively considered, the evidence did not support the jury's guilty verdicts on any of the charges made against Cardinal Pell.[107]

So how is this current law setting out when a court of criminal appeal may overrule a jury verdict relevant to whether jury verdicts should be sacrosanct?[108] The answer is that the High Court's statement of the law in *Pell* does not address that policy question.

Although the High Court has confirmed that a court of criminal appeal does not perform the same function as a trial jury when they objectively review the rationality of the verdict to which that jury came, in a Westminster system of government it is not the function of even apex courts to address policy questions like the continuing role of juries in criminal trial adjudication. That is the province of the legislature. While there have been recent questions about the wisdom of the non-availability of judge alone trials in criminal cases in Victoria,[109] that question has not

---

105   *Pell* (n 88) [37-38].

106   Ibid [39-40, 43-46, 91, 119, 125 and 127].

107   Ibid [125].

108   See for example Rick Sarre's discussion of the history of the inviolability of jury verdicts in "Why was George Pell's appeal successful when our justice system values jury verdicts?", *The Conversation*, April 7, 2020 <https://www.abc.net.au/news/2020-04-07/george-pell-appeal-jury-system/12129940>.

109   Farrah Tomazin and Sumeyya Ilaneby, "Andrews government considers 'judge-only' trials for criminal cases", December 13, 2018, <https://www.theage.com.au/national/victoria/andrews-government-considers-judge-only-trials-for-criminal-cases-20181213-p50m5u.html>. See also Greg Barns,

been permanently addressed by the Victorian legislature though judge-alone trials have been authorised during the Covid-19 crisis to deal with backlogs.[110] Felicity Gerry is not alone in questioning the wisdom of this move even on a temporary basis.[111] While she has acknowledged that research could be designed to "gauge the...fairness [of judge-only trials]", she noted research into "Diplock...judge-alone courts in Northern Ireland" had followed suggestions that those judges had become "'case-hardened' over time and thus biased against the accused", and that judges sitting alone in New South Wales in 2009 were much less likely to acquit than juries.[112]

In his Francis Forbes lecture in 2002, Ian Barker QC similarly defended the traditional English jury.[113] "Unchecked by juries, judges lose a connection with their community...[and become] easy prey to crusaders in the mass media".[114] Juries enable "'the people' [to be] seen as the ultimate source of power and authority in the Australian polity."[115] He observed that Lord John Russell traced the attachment of English people to their laws and trial by jury,[116] and that Lord Atkin said that juries had shielded "the poor from the oppression of the rich and powerful".[117] Barker also noted Priestley JA's retirement lament in New South Wales in 2001 that

---

"Everyone should have right to trial by judge, not jury", September 12, 2019, <https://www.smh.com.au/national/everyone-should-have-right-to-trial-by-judge-not-jury-20190821-p52j9i.html>, and Felicity Gerry, "Jury is out: why shifting to judge-alone trials is a flawed approach to criminal justice", May 5, 2020, <https://theconversation.com/jury-is-out-why-shifting-to-judge-alone-trials-is-a-flawed-approach-to-criminal-justice-137397>.

110   Gerry (n 104).
111   Ibid. She noted Lord Devlin's view that juries ensured liberty could not be crushed within the law and Sir Edward Bindloss' view that jury trials ensure citizen engagement in the administration of the law.
112   Ibid. Conversely there is the view that some persons accused of crime choose judge alone trials because their lawyers believe a jury would be completely unsympathetic.
113   Ian Barker QC, "Sorely tried, Democracy and trial by jury in New South Wales, Frances Forbes Lecture 2002, <http://www.forbessociety.org.au/wordpress/wp-content/uploads/2013/03/trial_jury.pdf>.
114   Ibid 23.
115   Ibid.
116   Ibid 29.
117   Ibid 30 quoting Lord Atkin's judgement in *Ford v Blurton* (1922) 38 TLR 801, 805.

the erosion of civil jury trials interfered with the spread of power into the community, and Dr HV Evatt's 1936 insistence that every adjustment to the jury system should be resisted "unless definitely proved to be necessary".[118] Barker also opined that Sydney Morning Herald attacks on the jury were the result of its "humiliation" in two jury defamation cases,[119] and yet his defence of the jury was grudgingly marred by the High Court's refusal to give the right to jury trial in s 80 of the *Australian Constitution* an interpretation consistent with the liberality accorded to the limited other rights there guaranteed.[120] But it is not clear why Barker thought that judges were more susceptible to media crusaders than jurors, and without an explanation, that belief discords with the scholarship noted above that asserts the contrary from the very beginning of the jury's life as an English institution.[121]

---

118   Ibid 31.

119   Ibid 253.

120   Ibid 233-238. For example, in *Attorney-General (Vic); Ex rel Black v Commonwealth (DOGs Case)* (1981) 146 CLR 559, Murphy J said that human rights guarantees should be interpreted liberally so as not to nullify the protection intended (ibid 622 and 631-634) and on that point Barwick CJ agreed with him (ibid 577) though Mason J suggested that since the religious freedom expressed in s 116 of the *Constitution* was expressed as a restriction on power, that liberal interpretation principle should not apply (ibid 614-615). However, the High Court has said that the guarantee expressed in s 51(xxxi) should be interpreted generously even though it practically restricts Australian Commonwealth power (*Minister of State for the Army v Dalziel* (1944) 68 CLR 261). The irony for Barker's argument is that despite being 'guaranteed' in the *Australian Constitution*, the High Court has found that there is no guarantee of jury trial anywhere in the Commonwealth, unless in Commonwealth criminal cases, the federal Parliament has made it legislatively clear that they intended a jury trial (see *R v Bernasconi* (1915) 19 CLR 620; *R v Archdall & Roskruge; Ex parte Carrigan and Brown* (1928) 41 CLR 128; *R v Federal Court of Bankruptcy; Ex parte Lowenstein* (1938) 59 CLR 556; *Li Chia Hsing v Rankin* (1978) 141 CLR 182; *Kingswell v The Queen* (1985) 159 CLR 264 and *Cheng v The Queen* (2000) 203 CLR 248).

121   For example, Thayer, *The Jury III* (n 9), has traced the way that the Executive sought to control juries from the 13th to the 17th centuries because their verdicts were so often regarded as perverse, and Green (n 43) has noted that jury conviction rates increased dramatically from the 16th century following Queen Mary's reforms (ibid 106-107). Thayer also explained that the process of attaint was gradually replaced by fine and then practically abandoned because it was unreasonable to punish jurors when they were simply called to infer their findings from decisions in open court (Thayer citing Vaughn CJ's decision when the jurors acquitted William Penn and William Mead at the Old Bailey in 1679, (n 9) 382).

The fact that jurors are no longer punished when they decide against the weight of evidence, does not present as a good reason why their decisions should be any more respected than those of a judge or a panel of judges. Nor does proof that some historical juries were punished for perverse verdicts respond to the view that their verdicts should not be appealable because they are a democratic manifestation of the will of the people. But the democracy insight does not answer the justice argument that those wrongly convicted should not be punished by the law. The existence of s 6(1) in the *Criminal Appeal Act 1912* (NSW) and s 276(1) of the *Criminal Procedure Act 2009* (Vic) which allow appeals against jury verdicts, show that those two legislatures have already determined that jury verdicts are not completely sacrosanct.[122] The legislative willingness to reform our laws of evidence also suggests that the democratic character of the jury has not entirely protected it from performance review.[123] It is submitted that s 276(1) of the *Criminal Procedure Act 2009* (Vic) as explained by the High Court in *Pell*, is sufficient to protect the innocent without the need to incur the time and expense of full jury retrial.

As already indicated, policy questions about jury reform are beyond the scope of this article. But the history of the jury here outlined, does justify reducing questions about 21st century jury retention and modification down to an analysis of two incommensurable ideas – whether the

---

122 Section 6(1) of the *Criminal Appeal Act 1912* (NSW) provides:
   The court on any appeal under section 5 (1) against conviction shall allow the appeal if it is of opinion that the verdict of the jury should be set aside on the ground that it is unreasonable, or cannot be supported, having regard to the evidence, or that the judgment of the court of trial should be set aside on the ground of the wrong decision of any question of law, or that on any other ground whatsoever there was a miscarriage of justice, and in any other case shall dismiss the appeal; provided that the court may, notwithstanding that it is of opinion that the point or points raised by the appeal might be decided in favour of the appellant, dismiss the appeal if it considers that no substantial miscarriage of justice has actually occurred.
   Section 276(1) of the *Criminal Procedure Act 2009* (Vic) provides:
   On an appeal under section 274, the Court of Appeal must allow the appeal against conviction if the appellant satisfies the court that—
   (a)   the verdict of the jury is unreasonable or cannot be supported having regard to the evidence; or   (b) as the result of an error or an irregularity in, or in relation to, the trial there has been a substantial miscarriage of justice; or   (c) for any other reason there has been a substantial miscarriage of justice.

123 Note that Thayer and Langbein both insist that the law of evidence is properly regarded as the law of jury control (Thayer, *The Jury III* (n 9) 388; Langbein (n 9) 317).

democratic contribution the jury makes to community justice is worth what that delivery costs. Properly understood, the history of the jury confirms that there is nothing sacred about the jury. Though juries in the past have acquitted some popular political prisoners,[124] and forced parliaments to adjust self-defence laws to allow manslaughter verdicts,[125] that history does not prove that judges whose impartiality and independence has been constitutionally protected since the beginning of the 18th century,[126] are any better at delivering just results in criminal trials in the 21st century.

Conclusion

Between the 12th and the 16th century the English jury was in a constant state of flux. In the 12th century, William the Conqueror used it to establish a taxation system and then to identify those who assassinated his occupying troops. A century later, Henry II used the jury to tighten up criminal justice so that people accused of serious crime could not escape standard criminal trial by calling on compurgators (character witnesses). Then a further fifty years later, Pope Innocent III's prohibition on

---

124   For example, in 1554, a jury acquitted Sir Nicholas Throckmorton for his part in Wyatt's rebellion and was punished by the court for a perverse verdict (Claire Ridgway, "17 April 1554 – Sir Nicholas Throckmorton's acquittal and an arrested jury", April 17, 2019, *The Tudor Society* <https://www.tudorsociety.com/17-april-1554-sir-nicholas-throckmortons-acquittal-and-an-arrested-jury/>). A century later, John Lilburne was similarly twice acquitted by a jury for inciting a rebellion against Cromwell (Lawrence MacLachlan, "The Trials of John Lilburne: Selected Links and Bibliography", *n.d.* <http://law2.umkc.edu/faculty/projects/ftrials/lilburnelinks.html>), and in 1670, William Penn was acquitted of unlawful assembly in *Bushell's case* and the Court of Common Pleas found it in appropriate to punish the jury for a perverse jury despite the trial judge finding that their verdict was a contempt of court (*Bushell's case* 1670 ER 1006).

125   Thomas Green, "The Jury and the English Law of Homicide 1200-1600" (1976) 74 *Michigan Law Review* 413.

126   The independence of the English judiciary is generally traced to the passage of the *Act of Settlement* (UK) in 1701 which fixed judicial salaries from the time of appointment and provided that judges could only be removed by the Crown after request by both houses of parliament. In Australia, that principle is reiterated in Chapter III of the *Constitution* and confirmed in a line of subsequent decisions including *New South Wales v Commonweath (Wheat Case)* (1915) 20 CLR 54, *R v Kirby; Ex parte Boilermakers' Society of Australia (Boilermakers Case* (1956) 94 CLR 254 and *Brandy v Human Rights and Equal Opportunity Commission* (1995) 183 CLR 245.

priestly involvement in any trial not conducted by the Church, saw the English jury further adapted to deliver final verdicts in criminal cases. In the 16th century, Queen Mary's bail and committal statutes finally began the process of bringing the jury under judicial control.

The story of the development of the English jury is a story of continuing evolution. While there were times when jury verdicts were unappealable, that misplaced sanctity was displaced in Australia by new statutes which allowed appeals when jury verdicts were inconsistent with the weight of the evidence and there was a possibility that innocent people had been convicted.

The bottom line is that even though juries ensure there is lay democratic involvement in the criminal judicial process, that does not mean our criminal justice system is perfect and cannot be improved. This brief summary of the history of some key points in the evolution of the English jury is intended to teach that the criminal justice system can always be improved including its jury elements. We should not be afraid to experiment with improvements. For as Oliver Wendell Holmes Jr famously observed in the 19th century,

> It is revolting to have no better reason for a rule of law than that it was so laid down in the time of Henry IV. It is still more revolting if the grounds upon which it was so laid down have vanished long since and the rule simply persists from blind imitation of the past.[127]

Understanding the history of the English jury should open our minds to reform possibilities.

---

127   Oliver Wendell Holmes Jr., *The Path of Law* (Bedford, Massachusetts, Applewood Books, 1897), 21.

Bibliography

A   *Articles*

Larry T. Bates "Trial by Jury after Williams v Florida", *Hamline Law Review* Vol. 10, No. 1 (1987) 53

Robert J East, "Jury Packing: A Thing of the Past?", 48(5) *The Modern Law Review* (Sept. 1985) 518

Thomas A. Green, 'The Jury and the English Law of Homicide', 1200-1600', (1976) 74 *Michigan Law Review* 413

Thomas A. Green, "The Transformation of Jury Trial in Early Modern England" in *Verdict according to conscience: perspective on the English criminal jury trial 1200-1800* (University of Chicago Press, 1985)

Roger A. Groot, "The Jury in Private Criminal Prosecutions before 1215", *The American Journal of Legal History*, Vol. 27, No. 2 (1983) 113

Roger A. Groot, "The Jury of Presentment before 1215, *The American Journal of Legal History*, Vol. 26, No. 1 (1983), 1

John H. Hatcher, "Magna Charta and the Jury System", *American Bar Association Journal* (1938) Volume 24, Issue 7, 555

R.H. Helmholz, "Compurgation and the Courts of the Medieval Church", *Law and History Review*, Vol. 1, No. 1 (1983) 1

R. H. Helmholz, "The Early History of the Grand Jury and Canon Law", *The University of Chicago Law Review*, Vol. 50, No. 2, Fiftieth Anniversary Issue (Spring 1983), 613

Naomi D. Hurnard, "The Jury of Presentment and the Assize of Clarendon", *The English Historical Review*, Vol. 56, Issue 223, (1941), 374

Clarance Ray Jeffery, "The Development of Crime in Early English Society", *The Journal of Criminal Law, Criminology, and Police Science*, Vol. 47, Issue 6 (1957) 647

John H. Langbein, "The Origins of Public Prosecution at Common Law", *The American Journal of Legal History*, Vol. 17, No. 4, 313

Peter T. Leeson, 'Trial by Battle', *Journal of Legal Analysis*, Vol.3, No. 1 (2011), 341

Finnbar McAuley, 'Canon Law and the End of the Ordeal', *Oxford Journal of Legal Studies*, Vol. 26, No. 3, (2006) 473

Robert C. Palmer, "Review: Conscience and the Law: The English Criminal

Jury Reviewed Work(s): Verdict According to Conscience by Thomas Andrew Green" (1986) 84 *Michigan Law Review* 787

Max Radin, 'The Privilege of Confidential Communication Between Lawyer and Client' (1928) 16(6) *California Law Review* 487

James B. Thayer, 'The Jury and Its Development I', *Harvard Law Review*, Vol. 5, No. 6, (1892), 249

James B. Thayer, "The Jury and Its Development III", *Harvard Law Review*, Vol. 5, No. 8, 357

Ralph V. Turner, "The Origins of the Medieval English Jury: Frankish, English or Scandinavian?", *Journal of British Studies*, Vol. 7, No. 2 (1969) 1

B   *Books*

R. Bartlett, *Trial by Fire and Water, The Medieval Judicial Ordeal* (Clarendon Press, 1986)

Harold Berman, *Law and Revolution: The Formation of the Western Legal Tradition* (Harvard University Press, 1983)

William Blackstone, *Commentaries on the Law of England* (New York and London, Garland Publishing Co., 1978)

Lord Devlin, *Trial by Jury* (Methuen, 1956)

William Forsyth, *History of Trial by Jury,* (John W. Parker and Son, London, 1852)

Thomas A. Green, *Verdict according to Conscience: Perspectives on the English Criminal Jury Trial 1200-1800* (University of Chicago Press, 1985)

William Holdsworth, *A History of English Law*, 2nd ed., (Boston, Little Brown and Co., 1923)

Oliver Wendell Holmes Jr., *The Path of Law* (Bedford, Massachusetts, Applewood Books, 1897)

John H. Langbein, *Torture and the Law of Proof, England and Europe in the Ancien Regime* (University of Chicago Press, 1976)

Diarmaid MacCulloch, *Thomas Cranmer, A Life* (Yale University Press, 1998)

F. W. Maitland, *The Constitutional History of England* (Cambridge at the University Press, 1919)

T.F.T. Plucknett, *A Concise History of the Common Law*, (Little Brown and Co., 5th edition 1956, Boston)

Frederick Pollock and Frederic William Maitland, *The History of English Law*, 2nd ed., (Cambridge University Press, 1968)

A. Keith Thompson, *Religious Confession and the Common Law* (Martinus Nihjoff, Leiden, 2011)

Nicholas Vincent, *Magna Carta, A Very Short Introduction* (Oxford University Press, 2012)

Paul Vinogradoff, *English Society in the Eleventh Century* (Clark, New Jersey: The LawBook Exchange Ltd, 2005)

C *Cases*

Attorney General (Vic); Ex rel Black v Commonwealth (DOGS Case) (1981) 146 CLR 559

Brandy v Human Rights and Equal Opportunity Commission (1995) 183 CLR 245

Bushell's case (1670) ER 1006

Chamberlain v The Queen (No 2) (1984) 153 CLR 521

Cheng v The Queen (2000) 203 CLR 248

Kingswell v R (1985) 159 CLR 264

Li Chia Hsing v Rankin (1978) 141 CLR 182

M v The Queen (1994) 181 CLR 487

Minister of State for the Army v Dalziel (1944) 68 CLR 261

New South Wales v Commonwealth (Wheat Case) (1915) 20 CLR 54

Pell v The Queen [2020] HCA 12

Pell v The Queen [2019] VSCA 186

R v Archdall & Roskruge; Ex parte Carrigan and Brown (1928) 41 CLR 128

R v Bernasconi (1915) 19 CLR 620

R v Federal Court of Bankruptcy; Ex parte Lowenstein (1938) 59 CLR 556

R v Kirby; Ex parte Boilermakers' Society of Australia (Boilermakers' Case) (1956) 94 CLR 254

D   *Legislation*

Act of Settlement 1701 (UK)

Crimes Act 1900 (NSW)

Criminal Appeal Act 1912 (NSW)

Criminal Procedure Act 1986 (NSW)

Criminal Procedure Act 2009 (Vic)

Magna Carta 1215 (UK)

Marian Bail Statute 1 & 2 Phil & Mary c. 13 (1554-1554)

Marian Committal Statute 2 & 3 Phil & Mary c. 10 (1555)

E   *Online materials*

Ian Barker QC, "Sorely tried, Democracy and trial by jury in New South Wales, Frances Forbes Lecture 2002, <http://www.forbessociety.org.au/wordpress/wp-content/uploads/2013/03/trial_jury.pdf>

Greg Barns, "Everyone should have right to trial by judge, not jury", September 12, 2019, <https://www.smh.com.au/national/everyone-should-have-right-to-trial-by-judge-not-jury-20190821-p52j9i.html>

BBC, Anglo-Saxon and Norman society pre-1066", *n.d.*, <https://www.bbc.co.uk/bitesize/guides/zq38tyc/revision/1>

BBC, "King John and Magna Carta", *n.d.* <https://www.bbc.co.uk/bitesize/guides/zqgqtfr/revision/2>

British Library, "William Marshal", *n.d.* <https://www.bl.uk/people/william-marshal>

The editors of Encyclopedia Britannica, "Petit jury", *n.d.* < https://www.britannica.com/topic/petit-jury#ref181484>

Felicity Gerry, "Jury is out: why shifting to judge-alone trials is a flawed approach to criminal justice", May 5, 2020, <https://theconversation.com/jury-is-out-why-shifting-to-judge-alone-trials-is-a-flawed-approach-to-criminal-justice-137397>

Paul Halsall, Fordham University, "Medieval Sourcebook: Twelfth Ecumenical Council: Lateran IV 1215, Canon 18 of the Fourth Lateran Council, March 1996. <https://sourcebooks.fordham.edu/basis/lateran4.asp>

"New revision of number 2267 of the Catechism of the Catholic Church on the death penalty – Resciptum 'ex Audentia SS.mi'", *Summary of Bulletin*, Holy See Press Office, 2 August 2018 < http://press.vatican.va/content/salastampa/en/bollettino/pubblico/2018/08/02/180802a.html>

Lawrence MacLachlan, "The Trials of John Lilburne: Selected Links and Bibliography", n.d. <http://law2.umkc.edu/faculty/projects/ftrials/lilburnelinks.html>

Papal Encyclical's Online, February 20, 2017, "Fourth Lateran Council: 1215", < https://www.papalencyclicals.net/councils/ecum12-2.htm>

Claire Ridgway, "17 April 1554 – Sir Nicholas Throckmorton's acquittal and an arrested jury", April 17, 2019, *The Tudor Society* <https://www.tudorsociety.com/17-april-1554-sir-nicholas-throckmortons-acquittal-and-an-arrested-jury>

Rick Sarre, "Why was George Pell's appeal successful when our justice system values jury verdicts?", *The Conversation*, April 7, 2020 <https://www.abc.net.au/news/2020-04-07/george-pell-appeal-jury-system/12129940>

Farrah Tomazin and Sumeyya Ilaneby, "Andrews government considers 'judge-only' trials for criminal cases", December 13, 2018, <https://www.theage.com.au/national/victoria/andrews-government-considers-judge-only-trials-for-criminal-cases-20181213-p50m5u.html>

Neda Vanovac and Dijana Damjanovic, "Azaria Chamberlain: Newly released NT cabinet documents detail decision to review convictions", January 1, 2017 *ABC News* <https://www.abc.net.au/news/2017-01-01/azaria-chamberlain-and-1986-cabinet-documents-released/8152774>

J. Willis, "Capital Punishment" in The Catholic Encyclopedia (New York: Robert Appleton Company, 1911) <https://www.newadvent.org/cathen/12565a.htm>

4

Should the jury be abolished in light of the High Court decision in the 'Pell' case?

Mark Bonanno

Introduction

On 11 December 2018, Cardinal Pell was found guilty of five charges related to the sexual abuse of two schoolboys. An earlier jury could not reach a verdict responding to the same charges. Four of these charges related to an allegation said to have taken place in late 1996 in the Cathedral against two boys referred to as A and B in the judgments. A is the only complainant while B although an alleged victim, had made no complaint and suicided some years past. The fifth charge related to a separate allegation of offending against A alone.

An appeal to the Victorian Supreme Court on 5 and 6 June 2019 was heard by Chief Justice Anne Ferguson, President of the Court of Appeal; Justice Chris Maxwell (who upheld the original decision); and Justice Mark Weinberg who dissented citing several grounds the most important of which was that the verdict was unreasonable.

The matter was then appealed to the High Court of Australia which heard the matter on 11 and 12 March 2020. The High Court quashed the convictions and acquitted the Cardinal on all five charges[1] by a unanimous decision of all seven judges on the basis that there was "a significant possibility that an innocent person has been convicted because the evidence did not establish guilt to the requisite standard of proof".[2]

If there are facts and circumstances which create a doubt and assuming that this doubt is a reasonable one, does that mean that the tribunal of fact (in this case the jury) cannot move beyond that fact and must conclude that the defendant is not guilty? Or considering the evidence, including the demeanour of the complainant, can the tribunal of fact conclude that the doubt has been removed?

This question must be viewed in the context of the history of the jury in England and Australia as the tribunal of fact. In the first part I will consider briefly the history of trial by jury and how our system of law has left jury verdicts as sacrosanct. Even on appeal, the verdict of the jury is not overturned. If it is found, for one reason or another, to be "unsound", then the appeal court moves to assuage the outcome by acquitting or ordering a retrial.

In some sense, the history of the laws of evidence over the past generation can be seen as an attempt to widen the field of inquiry allowed to the jury. In decisions like *IMM*[3] the High Court has allowed the jury to make decisions on some issues which had previously been the reserve of judges. The High Court there held that in determining the "probative value" of evidence under the *Evidence Act* a trial judge must proceed on the assumption that the jury will accept the evidence and no question as to the credibility or reliability of the evidence arises. In so doing the Court supported a more liberal rendering of the acceptance of evidence

---

1   *Pell v The Queen* [2020] HCA 12 (*Pell*).
2   *Pell* at [9] quoting the relevant test in *Chidiac, Chamberlain No2* and *M*.
3   *IMM v The Queen* [2016] 330 ALR 382.

than in Victoria favouring the NSW approach. In the second part I will consider this argument and conclude that far from being inconsistent the Court is consistently applying *IMM*. Indeed, it is acting in accord with its rulings since at least 1991.

In the third part I will consider cases where the tribunal of fact has made errors such as in *SY v R*[4] a case where the trial judge made directions which caused the jury to be misinformed. There are several other cases including High Court authorities since *Pell* which confirm how very high the bar is when considering the question of what lies "beyond reasonable doubt" and how this relates to jury verdicts.

Finally, in the fourth part I will consider some issues relating to jury trials and whether the *Pell* decision uncovers their inherent failings. Recent legislative changes introduced to eliminate jury trials for the duration of the COVID-19 outbreak may be welcomed by a grateful public and judiciary as measures we might profitably continue for the foreseeable future even after the pandemic is over. In that context is *Pell* the last nail in the coffin of juries as a long standing part of Australia's legal tradition?

Part One: The nature of appeals against jury verdicts

Indeed, we have approached our task by trying to put ourselves in the closest possible position to that of the jury.[5]

Ferguson CJ and Maxwell P hereby honestly set out their reasoning in the Victorian Appeal Court decision, and (inadvertently) the basis of their error. Jury decisions have been sacrosanct in the UK and Australia for hundreds of years. Indeed, the setting up of a Court of Criminal Appeal in the late nineteenth and early twentieth centuries both in England and Australia has exercised the minds of the legislature with no little

---

4   [2018] NSWCCA 6.

5   *Pell v The Queen* [2019] VSCA 186 [33].

controversy for that reason since that time.[6]

At that time jury verdicts were not to be overturned:

> Before the (*Criminal Appeal Act 1907*), the English criminal justice sys-
> tem did not provide for appeals on questions of fact. An appeal on
> a question of law was confined and could only be pursued with the
> leave of the trial judge. It may come as no surprise that leave was
> rarely granted. English judges were notorious for strong-arming ju-
> ries into returning the verdicts the judge wanted. It was thought,
> over-optimistically, that the Crown prerogative of mercy would be
> adequate to deal with the occasional wrongful conviction.[7]

How this played out in reality is demonstrated by *R v Snow*.[8] Snow was
accused of attempting to trade with the enemy under legislation enacted
at the beginning of the First World War. A jury was empanelled in the
South Australian Supreme Court before Gordon J. After 10 days listening
to documentary and other evidence, His Honour determined that there
was no case to answer. He so directed the jury, who then went out and
dutifully returned the appropriate verdict.

The matter before the High Court looked in part at whether His Honour's opinion of the law was correct. But more importantly, the jury
having already pronounced, could the verdict could be challenged?

In short, it could not. While Isaacs and Higgins JJ would have granted
leave to the prosecutor's appeal, the majority would not. Griffiths CJ
concluded that overturning the verdict was not open, even to the High
Court.

An appeal of a jury verdict under the *Criminal Appeal Act 1907* (UK) and

---

6   See a short history of the issue in The Hon Peter McLellan AM and Christopher
       Beshara, *A Matter of Fact: the Origins and History of the New South Wales Court of Crim-
       inal Appeal*, Education Monograph No 5, Judicial Commission of NSW, 1-12.
7   Ibid 3.
8   (1915) 20 CLR 315.

the Commonwealth and state Acts that followed it, did not make the appeal an opportunity for the superior court to reassess the evidence and come to a new conclusion. The appellate court's power was limited to determining if the jury had satisfactorily discharged their duty. Those judges could not superimpose new standards or reassess the facts. Likewise, the various iterations of the statutory provisions dealing with the nature of an appeal leading up to the current section which the Court dealt with in the *Pell* decision, s 276 of the Victorian *Criminal Procedure Act 2009*, all focus on the verdict of the jury being unreasonable or being incapable of support having regard to the evidence. It is not an exercise in re-examination of that evidence to the substitution of the later court's views.[9]

Another safeguard to ensure the validity of the jury's finding, set aside in some legislatures, is the need for unanimity of verdict.[10] Verdicts in most countries which follow the English jury tradition have required unanimous verdicts, and this was confirmed in *Cheattle* in cases under s 80 of the *Constitution*. Having twelve persons agreeing on a matter of guilt or innocence is itself a factor to assist an accused, rather than a prosecutor.

Perhaps the simplest expression of the test is found in the judgment of Barwick CJ in *Ratten*[11] - "If the court has a doubt, a reasonable jury should be of a like mind."

The jury are asked a simple question: Guilty or not guilty? Their reasons for determining the question one way or the other are unknown. This is important for another reason relevant to the *Pell* verdict. When reviewing a finding of unreasonableness by a jury we look at the directions given by the trial judge. Because the jury's reasoning is unknown, the polite assumption we (and the superior court) make is that if the jury made an unreasonable finding it was due to the failure of the trial judge's

---

9   Likewise, section 6 of the *New South Wales Criminal Appeal Act 1912*. Although all three pieces of legislation use differing formulae, they are very similar in impact.
10   *Cheattle v R* (1993) 177 CLR 541.
11   *Ratten v R* (1974) 131 CLR 510 [14].

direction. In part three we shall see more of that.

In *Pell* no such polite alternative recommended itself. The High Court called attention to the trial judge's directions and did not find them wanting.[12] Having so found, what other issues created an unreasonable verdict? Here we come to demeanour. What, if anything, can be made of the demeanour of the witness?

On appeal to a superior court, the answer is: nothing. In civil cases the court has found that civil juries and judges at first instance should be *guided* by demeanour only, and not be irreconcilably wedded to it.[13]

The error which manifested itself in the Victorian Court of Appeal was as follows: A[14] says the offending occurred. Fr Portelli says it probably did not.[15]

On that simple assessment as a statement of conflicting fact on the transcript alone there is a reasonable doubt.

Instead of merely reading the transcript, the appeal court looked at the original video evidence of A. Armed with the demeanour of A, the appeal court has additional data to make a conclusion that any logical contradiction is overcome. Portelli's assertion that it probably did not happen is met and defeated by A's heartfelt assertion that it did. The true test, based on objective fact and the transcript alone, has been thwarted.

By "entering the lists" and putting themselves as close as possible to the jury, the Victorian Court of Appeal went beyond the test which the legislation and the considerable body of law which followed it would have

---

12   *Pell* [31] where the Court extensively recounts the trial judge's directions to the jury exhaustively and thoroughly dealing with the defendant's forensic disadvantage in responding to allegations a quarter of a century old.

13   *Fox v Percy* 214 CLR 118 [129], cited in *Pell* [49].

14   The identification given to the complainant in all the *Pell* appeals.

15   Fr Portelli is one of the "opportunity witnesses" for which see later. As we shall see, the proposition is not as simple as this, but I cite this over simplification to demonstrate the error.

allowed.

Barwick CJ in *Ratten* does not invite the court to put itself in the jury's place and revisit the jury's finding. Nor did the previous s 568 of the *Crimes Act 1958* (Vic) with which he was dealing in *Ratten*; and nor does the current s 276 in the Act under which the *Pell* decision has been reviewed by the High Court.

The section only invites the appeal court to look at the whole of the evidence objectively and find if that determination by the jury was open to them, when they heard all the evidence.

The court on appeal then makes a declaration. If the verdict is sound, the consequence is dismissal of the appeal. If it is not, there are two options: acquittal or retrial. The jury's finding remains. The only question then is: what now follows?

Section 276 allows for more than just the unreasonableness of the verdict. The verdict might be unsound because of some procedural flaw[16] or due to a substantial miscarriage of justice.[17] The Court did not find that the video evidence was the reason for the flaw.[18]

Part Two: A contradiction from IMM?

So where did the jury (and the Victorian Court of Appeal) get it so wrong? In this we might at first instance see a contradiction between the High Court here and its determination in the matter of *IMM*.[19] In

---

16 *Criminal Procedure Act 2009* (Vic) s 276 (1) (b).

17 Ibid s 276 (1) (c).

18 There was much discussion in the case about the Victorian Court of Appeal's decision to view the video of witness A, the complainant. While finding that the video evidence should not have been viewed, this procedural irregularity did not sound as an additional reason for overturning that Court's decision. It is part of the unreasonableness. See below page 13ff.

19 *IMM*.

IMM the High Court appeared to have resolved a dispute between the NSW Court of Criminal Appeal[20] and the Victorian Court of Appeal.[21] All three cases are not about jury trial appeals in the same sense as *Pell*, but the High Court in *Pell* appears to be backtracking from its resolution in *IMM*.

Victoria and NSW are both subject to the *Uniform Evidence Act* and both cases deal with tendency (s 97) and coincidence (s 98) evidence, as well as the impact of the overriding s 137 dealing with the need for probative value of any evidence to outweigh any unfair prejudice.

The NSW approach as set out in *Shamouil* was to leave it to the jury to determine the reliability and credibility of such evidence subject to the proviso that s 137 may be invoked to prevent evidence going to the jury where it was obvious that the evidence was not reliable.[22] Other than that exception, it was open to the jury to review the evidence and make of it what they might.

Shamouil involved an appeal following a ruling by the trial judge that a recanted statement identifying the defendant should not be allowed into evidence. In finding that the evidence should be allowed in, Spigelman CJ specifically drew attention to the role of the jury in working out what to make of the evidence:

> To adopt any other approach would be to usurp for a trial judge critical aspects of the traditional role of a jury. In the case of evidence of critical significance, such a ruling by a trial judge would, in substance, be equivalent to directing a verdict of acquittal on the basis that the trial judge was of the view that a verdict of guilty would be unsafe and unsatisfactory. As the High Court said in that different, but not irrelevant, context in Doney v The Queen [1990] HCA 51; (1990) 171 CLR 207 at 275, this is not a permissible "basis for enlarging the powers of a trial judge at the expense of the traditional jury function". In my opinion, the same is true if a trial

---

20   In *Regina v Lenard Shamouil* (2006) 66 NSWLR 228 (*Shamouil*).
21   *Dupas v The Queen* (2012) 40 VR 182 (*Dupas*).
22   See *Shamouil* [63].

judge can determine the weight of evidence when applying s137.[23]

The Victorian Court of Appeal strongly disagreed. Credibility and reliability are salient in considering the evidence at "its highest and best", an expression and a formula the Victorian Court found in NSW authority.[24]

The *Dupas* case also involved identification evidence. The alleged offence took place in a cemetery. Dupas claimed to have no reason to be there as he had no relatives buried there (a claim which proved to be false); he had no alibi; other identity witnesses he claimed were in error; an admission he made to an inmate while in remand was, he claimed, false.

Credibility and reliability were, in the Victorian Court's assessment, central to this issue. These were not matters which could be left to a jury. They were evidence which needed to be assessed and screened by the Court, rather than left to a jury. The Victorian Court of Appeal specifically referenced *Shamouil* and called into question its conclusion.

> As we have said, the language of the statute and its context reflect a clear statutory intent that the test at common law should be maintained. That much appears to be generally accepted. The difficulty with Shamouil, in our respectful opinion, is that it proceeded upon a mistaken view of the traditional role of the trial judge at common law. Carusi, by contrast, accurately stated the common law position that the quality of the evidence was a matter to be taken into account in weighing the probative value.[25]

It was left to the High Court to resolve the contradiction in *IMM*. Here the evidence in question was a claim by the complainant (a child) that the defendant, during a massage had run his hand up her leg. This, argued the prosecution, evinced a sexual predilection in the defendant towards the complainant. Could this evidence be left to the jury to draw their own conclusion? The High Court majority (4:3) said yes, and specifically rejected *Dupas*.

---

23 *Shamouil* [64].
24 R *v Pearsall* (1990) 49 A Crim R 439.
25 *Dupas* [185].

> Once it is understood that an assumption as to the jury's accep-
> tance of the evidence must be made, it follows that no question
> as to credibility of the evidence, or the witness giving it, can arise.
> For the same reason, no question as to the reliability of the evi-
> dence can arise. If the jury are to be taken to accept the evidence,
> they will be taken to accept it completely in proof of the facts
> stated. There can be no disaggregation of the two – reliability and
> credibility – as Dupas v The Queen may imply. They are both sub-
> sumed in the jury's acceptance of the evidence.[26]

One might conclude that a High Court which came to this conclusion might be more open to leave the jury verdict in place in *Pell*. What hap-pened?

Firstly, *IMM* deals with what might be left to the jury to determine on their own, not the inherent unreasonableness or otherwise of the evi-dence. *Pell* involves the question of the conclusion, the verdict. Was the evidence set before the jury capable of yielding a verdict of guilty, not whether the evidence put before them would be improperly used.

Secondly, there is no contradiction between the High Court in *IMM* on the one hand and *Pell* on the other. *IMM* goes to giving the jury a larger amount of information than perhaps they had previously enjoyed, and certainly more than the Victorian Court in *Dupas* would have allowed.

What the High Court does is to consider what they then made of that evidence. A was a compelling witness, winning not only the jury's sym-pathy (if the verdict is anything to go by) but the Victorian majority's as well. The High Court's objection was whether, taking that evidence, and all of the other evidence as well, one can come to the conclusion of guilt beyond reasonable doubt.

One is tempted to opine that if A was compelling and truthful, then his version of the matter was to be preferred. This is not the test. With-

---

26   *IMM* [52].

out casting any doubt on A's veracity, can A's account, read with all the other evidence, result in a finding of guilt without positing a reasonable doubt? That is the real test, the test imposed by s 276 and all the law that has followed the review of jury verdicts since the *Criminal Appeal Act 1907* (UK).

The High Court, for reasons we will come to, found that it could not.

Indeed, without actually citing *IMM*, *Dupas* or *Shamouil*, I believe the Court actually dealt with this expectation and explained it succinctly and logically.

> The function of the court of criminal appeal in determining a ground that contends that the verdict of the jury is unreasonable or cannot be supported having regard to the evidence, in a case such as the present, proceeds upon the assumption that the evidence of the complainant was assessed by the jury to be **credible and reliable**. The court examines the record to see whether, notwithstanding that assessment – either by reason of inconsistencies, discrepancies, or other inadequacy; or in light of other evidence – the court is satisfied that the jury, acting rationally, ought nonetheless to have entertained a reasonable doubt as to proof of guilt. [27]

Credibility and reliability, the central questions in *IMM*, are assumed. Having accepted that, can the conclusion [verdict?] follow without raising a reasonable doubt? The High Court said no.

Indeed, an earlier panel of the High Court made much the same point in a case predating *Pell* by almost thirty years. As the High Court concluded in *Chidiac*:

> In resolving that question the court must necessarily recognize that issues of credibility and reliability of oral testimony are matters for the jury. For that reason, if for no other, an appellate court

---

27   *Pell* [39] (emphasis added).

will infrequently set aside a conviction as being unsafe because the evidence of a vital Crown witness lacked reliability or credibility. Nonetheless, occasions do arise when a jury proceeds to a conviction when the Crown case rests upon oral testimony which is so unreliable or wanting in credibility that no jury, acting reasonably, could be satisfied of the accused's guilt to the required degree. Then the appellate court must discharge its responsibility to set aside the conviction as one which is unsafe. When that happens the court is not substituting its view of credibility for that of the jury; the court is giving effect to its conclusion that, notwithstanding the jury's apparent willingness to accept the particular witness or witnesses as credible, the evidence was, having regard to its nature and quality, insufficient to satisfy a reasonable jury of the accused's guilt according to the criminal standard of proof.[28]

In fact, this assumption as to the credibility and reliability of the witness leads us to the first problem with the Victorian Court of Appeal's decision making in *Pell*: the use of the video evidence of A.

Central to placing themselves as close as possible to the position of the jury, the Victorian Court of Appeal allowed itself to view the video evidence of A. The High Court took the view that such action should only be taken in the most exceptional circumstances and for a "real forensic purpose".[29] This is because the jury is the trier of fact. On appeal it is for the judges to determine objectively whether the jury's reasoning supports the verdict. Of course we do not know the jury's actual reasoning, but the judge on appeal can and must make an objective review of the evidence to see if that conclusion was open.[30]

Is it not appropriate for the judges to put themselves in the shoes of the jury when viewing the evidence of the only witness to have seen all the facts leading to the charges? Again the High Court said no. Given what the High Court said above in relation to credibility and reliability, there

---

28   *Chidiac v R* (1991) 171 CLR 432 [27].

29   *Pell* [36].

30   See more on this later in *M* and *Libke*.

was no need. The jury could assume that the information presented by A was both credible and reliable. Pell was on trial, not A.

By viewing the video, the Victorian Court of Appeal ceased to act as an appellate court reviewing the evidence accepted by the jury as an objective exercise. Seeing the witness, being persuaded by his situation and his apparently compelling testimony, put the Victorian majority into the position of a second jury. This is not the Court's role. Far from exercising oversight, the Court was now trying to usurp the jury's function.

On the High Court's view there was no need to view the video evidence. There was nothing in it that could not be learned from a transcript. By viewing the video, the Victorian Court of Appeal was placing itself in the role of the jury, replacing the jury's assessment of the credibility of witness A. More importantly, by viewing the video they were open to the "highly subjective nature of demeanour based judgements".[31] Viewing the video was not merely a mistake, it exposed the Court to the charge of substituting its own view for that of the jury.

I note in passing that the High Court in an earlier decision, and in *obiter*, had presciently asked what might happen if video evidence were open to it;

> If it became routine for appellate courts to have access to a film or videotape of the trial, for example, it would probably be necessary to abandon the present rules of appellate review concerning demeanour.[32]

At very least we now know that the Victorian Court of Appeal was wrong and there is no need to abandon the rules on demeanour.

---

31   *Pell* [36 to 39].
32   Per McHugh J in *Fox v Percy* [89].

Part Three: The verdict of the jury is unreasonable or cannot be supported having regard to the evidence[33]

If we divide the *Pell* matter into two sets of allegations, the justification for finding the verdict was unreasonable becomes easier to understand. Charges one to four deal with one set of allegations relating to one day in, probably, December 1996 and concern an incident in the cathedral after mass.

Charge five deals with one allegation some months later where A claimed the Archbishop saw him in the company of other students and teachers; took him aside and groped him against a wall through his clothing.

The High Court in *Pell* does away with the defendant's 17 solid obstacles to conviction, which were in turn reduced to 13 by the time the appeal got to the Victorian Court of Appeal.[34] The High Court found that the obstacles were in fact three.[35]

The High Court also rejected an assertion that the Victorian Court of Appeal had reversed the onus of proof and imposed it on the defence. The High Court said the assertion that the defendant had to prove an impossibility was a mere "flourish".[36]

When all was boiled down, there was one witness, A, asserting strongly and compellingly that the offending happened. Against him stood 11 "opportunity witnesses",[37] not alleging that the offending did not happen, but unchallenged and suggesting that the offending was highly unlikely due to the various factual issues which they put concerning the usual practice of the Church; the usual practice of the defendant; the time it took for various actions by a multiplicity of persons to complete;

---

33   These are the terms of s 276(1) (a) of the *Criminal Procedure Act 2009* (Vic) which is the basis of the High Court acquittal.
34   *Pell v The Queen* [2019] VSCA 186 [408 and 409].
35   *Pell* [58].
36   Ibid [42]
37   Ibid [5]

the likelihood that persons would be at or near the place where the offending took place; and several other factors exhaustively dealt with in the judgement. It is hard to disagree with the conclusion of the High Court:

> Upon the assumption that the jury assessed A's evidence as thoroughly credible and reliable, the issue for the Court of Appeal was whether the compounding improbabilities caused by the unchallenged evidence summarised in (i), (ii) and (iii) above nonetheless required the jury, acting rationally, to have entertained a doubt as to the applicant's guilt. Plainly they did. Making full allowance for the advantages enjoyed by the jury, there is a significant possibility in relation to charges one to four that an innocent person has been convicted.[38]

That it could have happened is conceded. But that was not the test. Was there a reasonable doubt? Clearly, there must have been.

In terms of charge five, the circumstances were different. Here there were no timing issues, problems with the Archbishop being attended by others, problems with his clothing or the like. The alleged offence was simple: sometime after the first incident the Archbishop saw A and when other students and teachers were nearby, he took him aside and interfered with him through his clothing.

Surely here the jury were allowed to come to the conclusion they had made? Courts in unfair dismissal and sexual harassment cases regularly deal with allegations and offending not dissimilar to this, although usually by men against women. A President of the United States has boasted of doing precisely this to women.

Yet there remain several problems. The alleged offence was over twenty years old. According to A the offending took place before witnesses, both fellow students and adult teachers. There was no recollection by anyone of what would have been an unusual occurrence. No explana-

---

38   Ibid [119].

tion was provided by the prosecutor as to why there was no witness to explain this, or even to say that the Archbishop did or did not frequent the relevant hall.

The High Court concluded:

> In relation to charge five, again making full allowance for the jury's advantage, there is a significant possibility that an innocent person has been convicted.[39]

The High Court made it clear that the test imposed by M[40] was not one which required the Court of Appeal to find a path by which the jury verdict was possible, but a verdict that was capable of being made beyond reasonable doubt. In that regard the High Court removed any suggestion that the decision in *Libke*[41] created a contradiction. In their decision in *Pell*, the justices unanimously said:[42]

> As their Honours observed [in *Libke*], to say that a jury "must have had a doubt" is another way of saying that it was "not reasonably open" to the jury to be satisfied beyond reasonable doubt of the commission of the offence. Libke did not depart from M.

Having reconciled that matter, the High Court was able to say that obstacles remained between A's account and the rest of the unchallenged evidence which was before the jury at the hearing. As the High Court stated, there was "a significant possibility that an innocent person has been convicted because the evidence did not establish guilt to the requisite standard of proof".[43]

To demonstrate how high this standard is and also to show it is an error not confined to Victoria, the same High Court lacking only Nettle and Gordon JJ made a similar decision less than three weeks later.[44] In the

---

39   Ibid [127].
40   *M v The Queen* (1994) 181 CLR 487.
41   *Libke v The Queen* (2007) 230 CLR 559, in this context, the observation of Hayne J at 113.
42   *Pell* [45].
43   Ibid [9] citing *Chidiac, Chamberlain,* and *M*. Those citations omitted.
44   *Coughlan v The Queen* [2020] HCA 15.

Coughlan case, those judges dealt with a charge of arson and attempted fraud involving a fire at the defendant's house on Bribie Island in Queensland. He was found guilty by a judge and jury in the Brisbane District Court and he appealed to the Queensland Court of Appeal. Mr Coughlan had been seen running from his burning house by neighbours who knew him. He refused to stop and explain himself to the witnesses. He did later attend a police station to make a statement. Some of his clothing had evidence of accelerant (petrol) and he later made a claim against his NRMA insurance policy.

Coughlan's personal circumstances did not assist him. He admitted to severe mental problems which made him paranoid (which explained, he said, his running from the scene). These problems led him to act erratically and to have memory losses.

However, in giving his evidence he had posited a "bearded man" he had seen at the time. There was a reason for him being near his own property without being on it (selling a motorcycle entrusted to him by a friend for the purpose). The prosecutor did not explain or discharge its responsibility to eliminate this hypothesis and the scientific evidence of the smell of petrol on his clothes and person was not so overwhelmingly powerful to put the case beyond reasonable doubt in a circumstantial case. Finally, the insurance claim was significantly less than the value of the property lost making Mr Coughlan a very incompetent insurance fraudster if he was guilty as charged. The High Court concluded:

> It was not open to the jury to be satisfied of the appellant's guilt of either offence beyond reasonable doubt. The orders that the Court of Appeal should have made were those this Court made on 12 February 2020 quashing the convictions and entering verdicts of acquittal on each count.[45]

---

45   *Coughlan* [37].

A matter closer to the facts and allegations in *Pell* was SY.[46] SY, a novice Maronite priest, was accused of an offence occurring in 2005 and tried by a judge and jury in the District Court of New South Wales in 2015. The complainant was an altar boy 15 years old at the time of the alleged offence. Relics were on show at the Catholic Maronite Church at Croydon. SY is alleged to have invited the complainant to remain in the Church after hours. He was alleged to have invited the boy to travel with him to have a McDonald's breakfast in the late night or very early morning. The boy was said to be asleep and pretended to remain asleep when SY allegedly pulled the car over and interfered with him.

There were three grounds of appeal. The first was dismissed by the NSW Court of Criminal Appeal; the second dealt with a point relating to the rule in *Browne v Dunn* which was upheld; but the third issue – the unreasonableness of the verdict is relevant to the *Pell* matter. That ground for appeal was based upon s 6(1) of the *NSW Criminal Appeal Act 1912* which is the NSW equivalent of the provision dealt with in *Pell*.

The alleged unreasonableness was multifold: although the boy had reported the offending to friends and family members (all boys of his own age) only a few days after the events were alleged to have taken place, he still attended SY's ordination seven months later; was confessed by SY (a procedure requiring the penitent to be in an enclosed room with SY); and continued to attend mass and the sacraments with SY present. And there was also the question of why he did not simply show the novice that he was awake and push his hand away.

What was the explanation for this apparently inconsistent behaviour by the complainant?:

> Why? Why? I'll tell you why. I should stay, just stay calm. I'll tell you why. Firstly, you're a 15 year old boy and do you know what a priest is to me – was to me? He's like a, to, how does a 15 year old boy say no to God? How do you expect a 15 year old boy who's been raised as a good Christian Maronite who used to go to church

every single Sunday, every single church event – and I've lost all re-spect for it now because of this man – and you're telling me how do I say no to God? Sorry, but I, I was spiritual. I was very soft.[47]

Although the Court of Appeal made the distinction between SY as a priest and as a novice, one can understand the boy's sentiments.

A unanimous NSW Court of Criminal Appeal citing most of the author-ities the High Court relied upon in *Pell* came to this conclusion:

> However, in my opinion, a consideration of the evidence con-cerning the improbability of the events as asserted together with the evidence of the complainant's ongoing involvement with the church, the youth group and the applicant results in a conclusion that a reasonable doubt exists as to the applicant's guilt. That is a reasonable doubt which the jury ought to have had. That evidence ought to have caused them to scrutinise with some care the evi-dence of the complainant. However, the misdirections that result-ed from the impugned passages in the summing-up (relating to ground 2) are likely to have deflected the jury from that course.[48]

Placing all the elements together that Court weighed them all and notwithstanding the boy's earnestly felt emotions of shame and guilt could not reconcile them with all the facts. Much the same as the re-sult in *Pell*.

Part Four: the end of the jury?

Some supporters of the Cardinal have seen the jury's failure in the *Pell* decision as evidence that it is now time to do away with the institution of the jury.[49]

---

47   Ibid [90].

48   Ibid [102].

49   See for example Peter Hitchens, "The Decline of the Jury", in *First Things*, https://www.firstthings.com/web-exclusives/2020/04/the-decline-of-the-ju-ry?fbclid=IwAR2SI-UozRWyNwAppMjbB4HOnKP943gvGBnJC1b2MGh-g1QOk4-NDzgItTOQ? (Accessed 14 May 2020).

Without subjecting the matter to any legal analysis the idea of abandoning the jury in consequence of the result in the High Court in *Pell* is illogical.

Getting twelve disparate and unrelated people to unanimously agree[50] on anything, let alone guilt, is notoriously difficult. Presumably those circling the institution of the jury with pitchforks and torches want to commend the accused to the tender mercies of judges alone. Yet here the argument becomes more illogical. As set out above, two of three eminent judges in the Victorian Appeal Court were convinced of his guilt having put themselves in as close a position to the jury as they could.

The Queensland Court of Appeal made up of judges in *Coughlan* also "got it wrong" as did Judge Wass in the District Court of NSW in *SY*. Having the pronouncements of guilt or innocence made by a person wearing a wig and gown is no guarantee that the decision in such cases will be correct.

The point is justly made that the verdict appealed in *Pell* is the second chance a jury had to "get it right". The first trial ended in a hung jury. Should prosecutors be allowed to try and try again until they reach the answer they are seeking?

As a supporter of juries, the author suggests that the legislation could be amended so that a hung jury might be polled by the trial judge. Without nominating which jurors made which decision, the foreman of the jury would advise the Court that the jury were divided 6 all or 7:5 or 10:2. If unanimity was a close run thing with only one or two jurors disagreeing with the guilty verdict, an assumption might be made that the dissentient view was perverse.

If that were the case, the prosecutor would be allowed to press for a second trial.

---

50   See *Cheattle* (n 6).

If the division were more widespread, the assumption could be made that the evidence was not compelling and a reasonable doubt would be presumed, and no further trial permitted.

Perhaps the suggestion from those opposed to juries is that the judge alone could be assisted by another judge or judges. The same problem arises. Are three people in wigs and gowns more likely to come to a better conclusion on the facts?

Does the suggestion that serious cases be tried by multiple judges rather than lay jurors assume unanimity of response by more than one judge to the question of guilt or innocence? The point of unanimity is one derived from the centuries of law on jury trials not on verdicts of judges.

This is different from majority decisions in appeals. In an appeal the judges are looking to *legal* principle. They can and do give differing verdicts on legal issues. To take the notion of unanimity from the realm of the jury and apply it to judges appointed to deal with questions of fact is itself a misunderstanding of why jury verdicts must be unanimous. In many ways I am setting up a "straw man". I have seen no argument by those opposing jury trials indicating the need for unanimity by judges as the tribunal of fact. If this is what is proposed by them, I would argue that they are seeking to extend to the judiciary a rule which has its foundation in the centuries of jurisprudence which sought unanimity of jury verdicts. Majority verdicts are now allowed in many jurisdictions in a variety of circumstances. It would be a perverse outcome to remove jury trials, only to have judges assume the mantle of unanimity which is a hallmark of trial by jury at least historically.

Those who wish to abolish juries presumably want judges alone to determine matters. In that case, what answer do they give to the 2:1 decision in the Victoria Appeal Court? The above are reasons any lay person could give. If a jury can be in error, so can a judge, and with far more ease. If we subject the matter to the legal analysis prompted by the *Pell* verdict, there emerges an even stronger reason for preserving juries.

If we leave the matter to a judge alone as tribunal of both fact and law, we force the judge into a type of double think. The judge as tribunal of fact looks to the individual items of evidence assessing their reliability and credibility as set out above in *IMM* and the cases predating it.

Having completed that exercise the judge goes back to the evidence and as the tribunal of law then subjects the evidence to the test of M and the cases around that decision.

Yet that is not how judges (or juries) deal with the questions of fact before them, unless they are assessing an appeal. A judge alone will look to the evidence as it presents itself. If, for example, a judge has the question of Portelli's evidence that the accused usually was in a procession after the Mass, rather than in the presbytery, that fact is one which the judge weighs against A's testimony.

In an appeal, the judge or judges weigh several facts together, and can come to a conclusion about the likelihood of all the factors impacted by probability aligning together. The test of beyond reasonable doubt comes into play after the various chance elements are reviewed.

When the judge is the tribunal of fact and of law, the judge is making that assessment as she goes. As cited above, the Court could put itself *in the closest possible position to that of the jury.* Indeed, if we abolish the jury, that is precisely what the judge must do. The inherent unlikelihood of the offence which the High Court found would be overcome by the judge at first instance positing A against Portelli; and then A against every other opportunity witness. How that played out in reality in both the jury trial and the appeal Court is already known.

I would go so far as to say that if the matter were left to a judge alone rather than a jury, both Pell and SY would still be behind bars today. My evidence for that proposition is the decisions which judges made.

The High Court noted this two part exercise in the judgement itself:

> The function of the court of criminal appeal in determining a ground that contends that the verdict of the jury is unreasonable or cannot be supported having regard to the evidence, in a case such as the present, proceeds upon the assumption that the evidence of the complainant was assessed by the jury to be credible and reliable. The court examines the record to see whether, notwithstanding that assessment – either by reason of inconsistencies, discrepancies, or other inadequacy; or in light of other evidence – the court is satisfied that the jury, acting rationally, ought nonetheless to have entertained a reasonable doubt as to proof of guilt.[51]

Is it seriously doubted that a judge, in going about this exercise of both assessing the evidence as credible and reliable would not then be able to simultaneously assess the inconsistencies, discrepancies and other adequacies so as to confirm their initial positive assessment? A judge alone will be able to assuage any such problems in their initial assessment and come to a conclusion consistent with their findings on the evidence.

By allowing the judge alone to rule, the judge alone will prepare a far more compelling and consistent argument than one where they are merely adjudicating on someone else's verdict.

For those who are aghast at the jury verdict in *Pell*, the ability of the judge as tribunal of fact to consistently interpret the evidence with the question of reasonableness may have led to a verdict that was both contrary to the Cardinal's desired outcome and less open to challenge.

Conclusion

After the *Pell* verdict was delivered the ACT Supreme Court delivered a verdict on an interlocutory matter in *UD (No2)*.[52] Elkaim J was asked to rule on an application that an order not be made forcing the defendant

---

51   *Pell* [39] (emphasis added).
52   *UD (No2)* [2020] ACTSC 90, delivered 20 April 2020.

to submit to trial by judge alone. The ACT is one of several jurisdictions where the defendant may opt to be tried by a judge alone or a judge and jury. Special legislation has been brought down in the ACT and in all Australian jurisdictions to limit the availability of trial by jury for the length of the COVID-19 emergency.[53]

His Honour asked three questions, the second of which is relevant to us here: Can a judge alone trial be as fair to an accused as one before a judge and jury? His Honour gave a thorough and exhaustive review of the case law and learned articles on this question and came to the conclusion:

> Without any disrespect to the detailed arguments contained in the above judgments and articles I think the second of the three questions I posed above can be answered in this way: A judge alone trial can be a fair trial, but the decision on whether or not to order a judge alone trial has been influenced by the nature of the case and dictated by the wishes of the accused.[54]

His Honour's conclusion was that the trial can be fair absent a jury, a relevant question for the matter before him. He then went on to consider the accused's view of the matter against the public health considerations of the relevant COVID-19 legislation.

In my respectful submission the question posed by him and his thorough answer is not the end of the matter. The question is not whether the judge alone can deliver a fair trial but whether trial by jury as an institution should be continued.

My fear is that the "special circumstances" of COVID-19 might be the pretext to make the "emergency" into a permanent one. There are many opponents to the jury. Those supporting the Cardinal are only the most recent.

Doubtless criminal matters would be dispensed with faster and more

---

53   *Covid 19 Emergency Response At 2020* (ACT). All other jurisdictions have passed similar procedural acts.

54   *UD (No 2)* [41].

conveniently without juries. Judges and counsel could deal with complex and difficult matters without the need to dissect and explain matters to lay persons.

That for me is one of the institutional advantages of juries. We are a society that has said the people want to have a stake in how matters of guilt or innocence are determined. We want the facts broken down into comprehensible pieces that we the governed can assess and understand. We want to have confidence that justice is being done, not because someone in a wig and gown has assured us it is so but because the people who are governed by the system have had a part to play.

I do not for a moment understate the humiliation suffered by the Cardinal in being incarcerated for more than a year. The system (and juries are only one part of the "system") sometimes fails. Ask one of the many prisoners who have endured years if not decades in gaols unjustly accused and convicted and only released after DNA or some other evidence becomes available.

It would be tragic if dissatisfaction with the verdict in this one case, combined with the temporary emergency posed by COVID-19 were to rob society of an institution which has served us well for a millennium.

Bibliography

Legislation

Criminal Appeal Act 1912 (NSW)

Criminal Procedure Act 2009 (Victoria)

Criminal Appeal Act 1907 (UK)

Case law

Cheattle v R (1993) 177 CLR 541

Chidiac v R (1991) 171 CLR 432

Coughlan v The Queen [2020] HCA 15

Dupas v The Queen (2012) 40 VR 182

Fox v Percy 214 CLR 118

IMM v The Queen (2016) 330 ALR 382

Libke v The Queen (2007) 230 CLR 559

M v The Queen (1994) 181 CLR 487

Pell v The Queen [2019] VSCA 186

Pell v The Queen [2020] HCA 12

R v Pearsall (1990) 49 A Crim R 439

R v Snow (1915) 20 CLR 315

Ratten v R (1974) 131 CLR 510

Regina v Lenard Shamouil (2006) 66 NSWLR 228

SKA v The Queen (2011) 243 CLR 400

SY v R [2018] NSWCCA 6

UD (No2) [2020] ACTSC 90

Secondary Sources

Peter Hitchens, "The Decline of the Jury", in *First Things*, https://www.first-things.com/web-exclusives/2020/04/the-decline-of-the-jury?fbclid=IwAR-2SI-UozRWyNwAppMjbB4HOnKP943gvGBnJClb2MGhglQOk4-NDzgIt-TOQ? Accessed 14 May 2020

The Hon Peter McLellan AM and Christopher Beshara, *A Matter of Fact: the Origins and History of the New South Wales Court of Criminal Appeal*, Education Monograph No 5, Judicial Commission of NSW

Index

www.ingramcontent.com/pod-product-compliance
Lightning Source LLC
Chambersburg PA
CBHW061258220326
41599CB00028B/5695